BAHRAIN

Robert Cooper

MARSHALL CAVENDISH
New York • London • Sydney

Reference edition published 2001 by
Marshall Cavendish Corporation
99 White Plains Road
Tarrytown
New York 10591

© Times Media Private Limited 2000

Originated and designed by
Times Books International, an imprint of
Times Media Private Limited, a member of the
Times Publishing Group

Printed in Malaysia

Library of Congress Cataloging-in-Publication Data:

Cooper, Robert, 1945–
    Bahrain / Robert Cooper.
        p. cm. — (Cultures of the world)
    Includes bibliographical references and index.
    ISBN 0-7614-1161-5
    1. Bahrain—Juvenile literature.   [1. Bahrain.]   I. Title.
II. Series.
    DS247.B2 C66 2000
    953.65—dc21
                                        00-043116
                                           CIP
                                           AC

INTRODUCTION

THE STATE OF BAHRAIN is a group of 33 small islands set in the the Persian Gulf off the northeast coast of Saudi Arabia. The country's main island, also called Bahrain, is linked by a bridge to Saudi Arabia.

Bahrain is the only country in the Gulf that has more citizens than guest workers. There are three Bahrainis for every two non-Bahrainis, and Muslims, mostly Shiites, form 85% of the population. Although oil production started in Bahrain in 1932, before anywhere else in the Arab world, the economy today relies less on oil production than on industry. Bahrain, an absolute monarchy, is the only Gulf state to adopt a strict rule of primogeniture for the ruling royal family.

Together the islands of Bahrain compose an area of 267 square miles (692 square km), about the size of the Republic of Singapore. Independence from Britain was achieved in 1971. Since then, Bahrain has forged a unique Bahraini identity.

CONTENTS

The wooden carvings on this door depict the typical symmetry found in traditional Bahraini architecture.

CONTENTS

Popular silver accessories worn by Bahraini women include intricate armlets such as the ones above.

GEOGRAPHY

BAHRAIN IS A LOW-LYING ARCHIPELAGO of 33 islands (including the disputed Hawar group) set in the Persian Gulf. The sheikhdom sits 15 miles (24 km) off the east coast of Saudi Arabia and 17 miles (27 km) from the west coast of Qatar. Located north of the Tropic of Cancer, Bahrain shares the same latitude with Miami and the same longitude with Tehran, the capital of Iran.

Bahrain Island, the largest island in the archipelago, measures 30 miles (48 km) by 10 miles (16 km). It is connected by causeways to the next biggest islands—Al-Muharraq and Sitrah. Al-Muharraq, located off the northeast tip of the main island, is the site of Bahrain's famous international airport, and the smaller, largely industrial Sitrah is located off the east coast of Bahrain Island. Apart from these three well-connected islands, none of the remaining 30 are of significant size.

Left: **This new causeway links the capital of Bahrain, Manama, to Saudi Arabia.**

Opposite: **An oasis in a desert of Bahrain supports the growth of date palms and enables the survival of animals such as camels.**

Surrounded by water, Bahrain's location and good harbors were central to its centuries-old role as an entrepôt or a center of trade. This continued until recently with the airport providing a convenient and efficient refueling stop for long-haul air travel between Europe and the Far East. While the airport remains one of the world's most important in terms of total traffic, most of Bahrain's visitors arrive by motor vehicle via the 16-mile (26-km) causeway linking Umm an Na'san Island, off Bahrain's west coast, to Saudi Arabia.

THE IMPORTANCE OF WATER

Bahrain has the same climate as the other Gulf states. It is hot and humid with little rainfall. The significant advantage for Bahrain is the existence of substantial ground water and many natural springs. Along with its good

Only 1% of Bahrain's land is arable, made possible through irrigation.

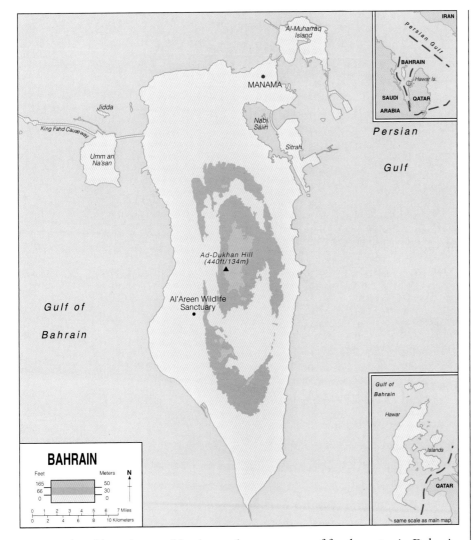

There are no permanent rivers in Bahrain.

geographical location and harbors, the presence of fresh water in Bahrain attracted trading vessels in the past because the merchants regarded the land as a convenient oasis in a desert.

It was the existence of drinking water that allowed the ancient culture of Dilmun to take root and prosper on the comparatively fertile shores in the north of Bahrain about 5,000 years ago. The Al-Khalifas, Bahrain's present-day ruling family, left the Arabian mainland and established themselves in Bahrain in the 18th century because Bahrain had an adequate supply of fresh water.

The Arabian Oryx is one of the few animals that thrives in Bahrain.

FLORA AND FAUNA

For a long time Bahrain has been famous for its greenery at the heart of the Gulf region's deserts. Archeological scholars have attempted to locate the mythical Garden of Eden in Bahrain, and books have been written on the flowers of Bahrain.

Just how green Bahrain was in antiquity will probably never be known. What is certain is that it is less green now than it used to be. Bahrain's famous underground springs, which water the trees and flowers and gave Bahrain the epithet "Land of a million date palms," have been so strained by demand that the plantlife they support are decreasing.

Compared to its barren neighbors, Bahrain may be green, but on a world scale, its flora contains little of interest to the international botanist. The same can be said for the fauna. Even the camel, ubiquitous throughout the Middle East, is an imported rarity in Bahrain. Apart from the domestic donkey, there are very few animals to be seen in Bahrain.

One place where animals are more commonly seen is the Al'Areen Wildlife Sanctuary. Six miles (10 km) long, this conservation area houses more species that are indigenous to Arabia than to Bahrain, such as the Arabian Oryx. The authorities also introduced zebras to the sanctuary. They are said to have adapted well to the local conditions and, like most immigrants to Bahrain, seem to have thrived in their new home.

The most interesting aspect of Bahraini fauna is found underwater, off Bahrain's comparatively long coastline. Thousands of years before the Bahrainis struck oil, they prospered by exploiting an abundance of pearls and fish.

Pearling is a tourist nostalgia and romance industry today, and the oysters and their pearls remain undisturbed on the seabed. Fishing remains an important occupation in a country committed to minimizing the import of foodstuff. The sea adds variety to Bahraini cuisine and, for a comparatively small investment, provides a man and his family with an independent and prosperous livelihood.

LAND OF A MILLION DATE PALMS

Bahrain is referred to in old records as the "Land of a million date palms." Bahrainis consider the date palm to have been blessed by God with qualities not found in other trees. Everything from it is useful: the dates provide food for people and domestic animals; the trunk and branches are used for building houses, boats, and fish traps; the leaves are used to weave mats, fans, and baskets; the fibers are twisted into ropes; and the wood provides a valuable source of fuel.

Temperatures in Bahrain can go as high as 120°F (48°C) in the summer, especially in the desert region.

CLIMATE

Bahrain is very hot and humid during summer. From April to October temperatures range from 86°F (30°C) to 120°F (48°C), with the average daytime temperature between June and September running at a steady 97°F (36°C).

Winter, which lasts from November to March, is cooler, with temperatures varying between 57°F (14°C) and 77°F (25°C). The weather from December to February is the most pleasant, with temperatures averaging 63°F to 66°F (17°C to 19°C). Humidity remains high all year.

Rainfall between June and October is practically nonexistent. The winter months are the wettest, although wet in the Bahraini sense means an average of only 3 inches (76 mm) of rain a year.

The climate varies little throughout Bahrain because the country is small and has no highlands. Today most of the buildings in the country are air-conditioned during the hottest months. Bahrainis also join tourists in the resorts in Manama to escape the summer heat.

CITIES

Modern cities in Bahrain are clean and functional. Built to provide relief from the heat, shopping centers, hotels, and clubs provide air-conditioned sanctuary from the midday sun. The modern city is fashioned after the *suq* ("SOOK"), a popular and busy marketplace with narrow and maze-like streets. The *suq* used to be the commercial heart of the city. Sadly for many older Bahrainis, the *suq* has been replaced by air-conditioned centers since the 1960s. The original streets have made way for comfortable housing blocks and office complexes. There are few traditional *suq* left in Bahrain.

Many buildings in Manama, Bahrain's capital, stand on reclaimed land.

HISTORY

FOR AT LEAST 7,000 YEARS people have lived in Bahrain. Stone Age Man lived here from 5000 to 3000 B.C., enjoying a diet rich in seafood. With no evolutionary break suggested by invaders or migrants and undisturbed by war or resource scarcity, one of the earliest and most peaceful cultures developed. It is now known to the world as Dilmun.

THE STONE AGE

From 5000 to 3000 B.C. fishermen and hunters lived peacefully on Bahrain's islands. During this period, the inhabitants made their tools and weapons from locally available materials—stone, bone, and wood. The first Bahrainis had an advantage over other Stone Age people because flint, which is easier to make into sharp and piercing tools, is readily found embedded in the limestone layers of Bahrain. These tools, in the form of

Left: **Qal'at al-Bahrain, also known as Bahrain Fort or Portuguese Fort, is the main archeological site in Bahrain.**

Opposite: **This carving, displayed at the Bahrain National Museum, depicts the legend of Dilmun.**

15

An archeological site of an old settlement.

arrowheads, knives, and scrapers, have survived to the present day as evidence that Bahrain was occupied during the Stone Age.

Technology at this time was so simple that every man made his own tools. There was no need for exchange or commerce and, in Bahrain there was no need to come together for defense or hunting. Animals were probably not serious threats to the early Bahraini, who hunted comparatively small game. The extended family was sufficient to provide the labor required.

Remains indicate that Stone Age settlements existed on several of Bahrain's islands. How these settlers crossed the 15 miles (24 km) of water from Arabia remains unknown. Early vessels used to navigate to Bahrain or move between islands were most likely made of either wood or bundles of rushes, and all have perished over time.

It has been suggested that 4,000 years ago, when the straits separating Bahrain from Arabia were narrower, natural causeways might have been exposed during low tide to allow passage. The evidence of human settlements in Bahrain tends to support this theory. The modern, man-made causeways which are so vital to the prosperity of today's Bahrain perhaps have natural prototypes that first allowed the islands to become inhabited.

This Early Type grave showed that people were buried in a sleeping position with decorative and useful items, indicating a belief in afterlife.

THE FORMATIVE DILMUN ERA

During 3200 to 2200 B.C., the extended family groups of Stone Age hunter-gatherers in Bahrain evolved into a complex agricultural and urban civilization known as Dilmun.

At that time there were no nation states as we know them today. However, historians are certain Dilmun covered an area much greater than the present national boundaries of Bahrain.

The archeological evidence discovered in Bahrain is mostly found in Early Type graves, which date from 2800 to 2200 B.C. Analysis of grave findings suggests a culture that had connections with other parts of the Middle East. While the most common find was plain, locally made pottery, which was the forerunner of the special Dilmun ware, there was also some exquisite, painted pottery. These pots resemble those found in the southern part of the Gulf.

Other discoveries that suggest cultural exchange include a copper dagger made from copper imported from Oman, carnelian beads from the Indus Valley, and round-bottomed pots originally from Mesopotamia.

Stamp-seals found in some graves are taken as a sign of the increasing importance of commerce and trading.

THE NATURE OF DILMUN SOCIETY

Dilmun is depicted as an ancient trade center linking Mesopotamia and Syria in the north, the Indus Valley in the east, Baluchistan and Kurman in Iran, Arabia and Egypt to the west, and Oman in the south. Dilmun presented a trader's oasis to all these countries, and goods were exchanged within Dilmun's boundaries.

Dilmun was not, however, simply a service port. Its citizens were very active in a vast trading area with a great range of products. In fact, the degree to which they excelled in commerce and maritime activity has been taken as a distinctive feature of Dilmun.

In addition to its strategic geographical position and ample sweet-water springs, Dilmun's peaceful character was important to its international trade. From what historians can determine, Dilmun never engaged in wars. It survived, Switzerland-like, because its surrounding giant nations needed its services. Like Switzerland, Dilmun remained neutral from the various conflicts that surrounded it, peaceful but certainly not passive. Archeologists have uncovered many weapons over the years as proof that Dilmun was a military power.

There is, however, one intriguing aspect of Dilmun culture that remains to be explained—the depiction of naked soldiers on Dilmun seals. Dilmun's soldiers are often as not depicted naked although none of the cultures that most influenced Dilmun (Mesopotamia, Egypt, and Indus) had naked soldiers. The number of soldiers Dilmun had, or whether they went naked, will probably never be known. What is certain is that Dilmun's ability to defend itself, along with the advantages a neutral Dilmun offered its trading partners, maintained Dilmun as a culture whose interests lay in peace, but which stood ready to defend itself should the need arise.

The study of bones and teeth of early Bahrainis suggests they ate fruits, vegetables, meat, fish, and few grain products. The diet changed about the time Islam was introduced. Grain products such as rice and bread subsequently formed the major part of the diet.

SEALS

Among the most significant excavated artifacts are the famous Dilmun seals that, similar to ancient chops found in the Orient, are a form of signature. A man would use a seal to set his mark to an agreement. When he died, the seal would be buried with him.

SHELL SEALS Made from cone shells, the first seals were in use in the Late Formative and Early Dilmun periods (2400 to 1800 B.C.). The natural coils of these shells are as unique as human fingerprints and were accepted as identity marks. The top of the shell would be cut off and the underside smoothed to serve as a printing face. A copper ring would be attached to the reverse side to facilitate imprinting. To the untrained eye, they closely resemble the stone seals which emerged later.

STONE SEALS The making of the first stone seals overlapped the use of shell seals. Measuring 0.7 to 1.4 inches (1.8 to 3.6 cm) in diameter, these circular seals are unique to the Dilmun culture. Animals, usually bulls and antelopes, were carved on one side with the reverse inscribed with three lines flanked by four encircling dots to represent the eyes of the Sun God.

SEALS AND THE SUN GOD

It has been hypothesized that like Mesopotamians, Phonecians, and inhabitants of the Indus Valley, the people of Dilmun worshipped a Sun God. It is thought that the central coil of the shells, along with engraving lines that radiate to the circumference, symbolized the sun. Some seals were further individualized by a series of small holes drilled around the periphery of the shell. These tiny holes are believed to represent stars.

WHAT THE SEALS SAY

The designs of the Dilmun seals bear a remarkable resemblance to seals found from the Indus Valley to Mesopotamia. The seals were also used in the same manner, suggesting early interaction between these similar civilizations.

Made with simple tools, many seals contain a religious motif. The Sun God was a common motif, represented by bulls with human heads and torsos. Enki, the God of Pure Water, was also popular, usually symbolized by water carriers and the star sign. Other deities are also represented, usually seated on a throne and wearing a horned crown, the sign of divine power. Such religious ideas and their depiction were common in the Gulf, and these strongly point toward some form of cultural exchange with ancient Mesopotamia.

The depiction of swords, shields, harpoons, spears, shields, bows, arrows, and warships on seals suggests that Dilmun was a military power with an impressive collection of weapons. The engraving of naked soldiers on seals reveals that Dilmun regarded its soldiers as heroes and respected them nearly as much as they worshiped their gods.

Around 2000 B.C. a completely new style of stone seal emerged. Unlike the earlier seals, which were known for their individuality, these stone seals were numerous and so standardized that they appear to have been the license authorizing certain individuals in Dilmun to act as merchants and officials. As the Gulf area began trading activities, Dilmun seals became known and respected from India to the Mediterranean.

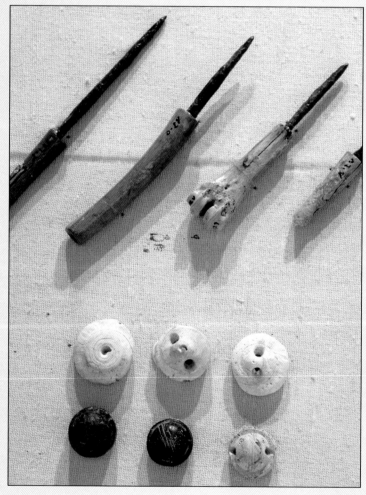

EARLY DILMUN

Dilmun reached its zenith between 2100 and 1700 B.C. During this period, an early trading site at Qal'at al-Bahrain, located in the fertile north of the island, developed into a major city. There, a population of between 2,000 and 4,000 people carried out functions mostly related to commerce and defense. Remains of what was probably a palace suggests a ruler of royal status, although there are no written records of the type of authority structures that existed before 1780 B.C.

Significant labor went into the construction of graves, marked by burial mounds at A'ali, and many thousands of mounds continue to form a prominent feature of Bahrain's landscape.

In addition to being a prosperous trading center, Dilmun was considered a sacred place. Worship was centered in the northwest corner of Bahrain, where five temple complexes were located and freshwater springs are the most abundant. The architecture of these temples suggests shared religious ideas in the Gulf region.

Prehistoric burial grounds are found throughout Bahrain, making it one of the largest ancient graveyards in the world.

MIDDLE AND LATE DILMUN

During the years 1600 to 1000 B.C., Dilmun became increasingly influenced by the outside world. Potters continued to use Bahraini clay and traditional methods of preparation but imitated the styles and shapes of Mesopotamian pottery. Around 1400 B.C. Kassite kings of Babylon took control of the islands, repaired the city walls at Qal'at al-Bahrain and built massive stone storehouses for warehousing and distributing goods.

Dilmun continued to be part of the Gulf trading and business community, but hundreds of years passed without any mention in Mesopotamian written sources.

As Dilmun's population and urban-type settlements expanded into the Iron Age, the Late Dilmun period seems to have been marked by a gradual decline in international influence.

A Late Dilmun burial necklace on display at the Bahrain National Museum.

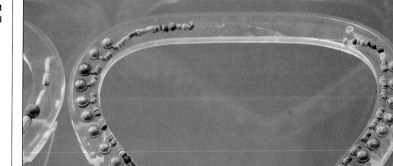

Tylos pottery at the Bahrain National Museum.

TYLOS

From 331 to 323 B.C. Alexander the Great extended Greek influence in the wake of his conquests to the north of Bahrain. Greek administration, language, art, and culture were introduced in these areas. Dilmun was full of merchants and imports from Greece. Even the name Dilmun was changed to the Greek "Tylos."

Intending to secure Arabia within his growing empire, Alexander sent his admirals to inspect the various Gulf islands and peninsulas. According to their reports, Tylos was an agricultural land, mostly unwooded, with cotton trees, fine fabric production, wood suitable for shipbuilding, and magnificent pearls. More important, the islands were praised for their plentiful sources of good water.

Tylos would have been part of Alexander's conquests in Arabia if he had not died in 323 B.C., three days before the invasion. By this time, Greek influence in Tylos had extended to language, and housing styles had changed—there were now courtyards and flat roofs.

The Arad Fort on Al-Muharraq guards the south harbor of the island. Built around the 16th century, the fort was fortified by the Portuguese during their rule in Bahrain.

THE COMING OF ISLAM

In A.D. 629 Prophet Mohammed invited the Bahrainis, then known as Awal, to convert to Islam. Many converted, and within a few years Bahrain became a center for the spread of Islam, undertaken peacefully through contacts made by trade. The Koran was soon an item found in most houses.

CENTURIES OF DISPUTE

In the 15th century Bahrain avoided military confrontations with the Portuguese, who were intent on dominating sea trade. The country also avoided the violent struggles between the Ottomans, the ambitious Persians, and well-armed European powers.

In the early 16th century Bahrain was conquered by the Portuguese. They ruled Bahrain until 1602. The country then survived under a series of Persian rulers until the end of the 17th century. In 1718 Oman seized Bahrain from the Persians and held it until 1737, when Persia recaptured it. The next period was the most chaotic time in Bahrain's history. Independent sheikhdoms fought for control of the islands. This lasted until 1783 when Bahrain was conquered by the ancestors of the present ruling family, the Al-Khalifas.

THE AL-KHALIFA FAMILY

The modern history of Bahrain is inextricably tied to the history of the Al-Khalifas, who were originally part of a confederation of Arab tribes known as the Utoob. The Al-Khalifas migrated from Arabia to Bahrain in 1701. Sheikh Ahmed bin Mohammed Al-Khalifa, who became ruler of Bahrain in 1783, started the uninterrupted rule of the Al-Khalifa family.

SHEIKH ISA BIN AL-KHALIFA (1869–1932)

Sheikh Isa was 21 when he became the seventh Al-Khalifa ruler in December 1869, after Britain stepped in to put an end to family squabbles over who was to become ruler. As emir, Sheikh Isa introduced new administrative and legal institutions and laid the foundation for modern education before he died in 1932. In 1881 and 1891 he signed two agreements which reinforced British control in Bahrain. During his reign, imports and exports increased dramatically; Bahrain's first bank and post office were opened; and a telegraph station linked the island-state to the rest of the world.

SHEIKH HAMAD BIN ISA AL-KHALIFA (1932–1942)

Sheikh Hamad's reign saw a decade of important firsts—the first telephone in 1932, cinema in 1938, newspaper in 1939, radio station in 1940, and census in 1941. The discovery of oil, one of the most significant events in Bahrain's history, took place in 1932. Following that, Britain moved its main naval base in the Gulf to Bahrain in 1935. Land reclamation to increase the size of the country started in 1924 on the Manama Sea Road. The first commercial airplane landed at Manama in 1932, and by 1941 the causeway that links Al-Muharraq Island to the main island was completed.

SHEIKH SALMAN BIN HAMAD AL-KHALIFA (1942–1961)

Sheikh Salman laid the foundation for Bahrain's peaceful independence from Britain. To ensure that Bahrain's progress would not be sacrificed in an unprepared rush for independence, he geared the nation toward full modernization. In 1949 piped water was introduced to Manama. Three years later the emir gained jurisdiction over all Gulf nationals living in Bahrain. In 1956 Sheikh Salman established the Administrative Council, which later became the Council of Ministers.

H.H. SHEIKH ISA BIN SALMAN AL-KHALIFA (1961–1999)

Sheikh Isa, the father of Bahrain's independence, was born June 4, 1933, the eldest son of Sheik Salman. He became head of Manama Municipality in 1956 and crown prince in 1957. After his father died in 1961, Sheikh Isa became emir and remained ruler until his death in 1999. Under his leadership, Bahrain achieved independence on August 14, 1971 and became a member of the United Nations the same year. Sheikh Isa also played a significant role in the creation of the Arab Gulf Cooperation Council in 1981. Building on the base of a modern state, Sheikh Isa's administration greatly improved the country's infrastructure. The Manama-Sitrah and the Saudi causeways were opened in 1986.

GOVERNMENT

BAHRAIN'S SYSTEM OF GOVERNMENT is most often described as an absolute monarchy, sometimes with the adjectives "benevolent" or "enlightened" attached. The line of authority follows the male line of the Al-Khalifa family, with each ruler remaining in power until his death, when power is passed to his male heir, the eldest son. The heir will usually have years of apprenticeship before taking control, the usual pattern being for him to serve as deputy or in another authority position until it is time for him to accept responsibility to work for the welfare of Bahrain.

The Al-Khalifas can be seen as a large extended family. The words "clan" and "tribe" have been used to describe this kinship unit from which Bahrain's leaders are exclusively drawn.

On some occasions in the past there were conflicting views and discords as to who should assume the leadership. To remove this source of potential disharmony, Bahrain has adopted strict rules of primogeniture

Left: **Sheikh Isa bin Salman Al-Khalifa, emir from 1961 to 1999, awarding prizes at a sports competition.**

Opposite: **The Pearl Monument is a tribute to the pearl divers who had contributed significantly to Bahrain's prosperity in the past.**

27

for the royal family. This means that the eldest son is heir and only when he dies without male descendant can a second son assume control. Bahrain is the only country in the Gulf to have adopted the law of primogeniture to control the royal succession. The rule is in line with Islamic ideas on inheritance and ensures clarity and transparency regarding where the power lies and will lie in the future.

The current emir or ruler of Bahrain, Sheikh Hamad bin Isa Al-Khalifa, does not rule alone. He regularly consults with government ministers and is known to be readily available to citizens. The heir apparent is Crown Prince Salman bin Hamad.

Below: **Britain's Queen Elizabeth receiving Emir Sheikh Hamad bin Isa Al-Khalifa during an audience at Buckingham Palace in London on November 23, 1999.**

THE IMPORTANCE OF THE AL-KHALIFAS

Sheikh Hamad bin Isa Al-Khalifa, who became emir in 1999, was head of the Bahraini defense forces during his years as crown prince. The prime minister of Bahrain, Sheikh Khalifa bin Salman Al-Khalifa, is the emir's uncle. Sheikh Mohammed bin Mubarak Al-Khalifa is Minister of Foreign Affairs. Sheikh Mohammed bin Khalifa Al-Khalifa is Minister of Interior. Sheikh Khalifa bin Ahmed Al-Khalifa is Minister of Defense. Sheikh Abdulla bin Khalid Al-Khalifa is Minister of Justice. Sheikh Ali bin Khalifa Al-Khalifa is Minister of Transportation. Sheikh Khalid bin Abdulla Al-Khalifa is Minister of Housing, Municipalities, and Environment. Sheikh Isa bin Ali Al-Khalifa is Minister of Oil and Industry. Sheikh Isa bin Rashid Al-Khalifa is President of the General Organization for Youth and Sports. Those in ambassadorial positions overseas are most likely to come from the eminent Al-Khalifa family.

INTERNAL SECURITY AND NATIONAL DEFENSE

Even under British protection, internal security was largely regarded as a matter for the ruling Al-Khalifa family. With full independence, the country's defensive security is also the responsibility of the ruling family. The Minister of Defense is an Al-Khalifa, the emir is supreme commander, and the crown prince is commander of the Bahrain Defense Force.

In the wake of the 1990 Gulf War and the internal dissent from 1994 to 1996, Bahrain's defense forces have been strengthened with the launching of the Trigate Sabha and the Emiri Decree of January 7, 1997, which provided for the formation of a National Guard under Sheikh Mohammed bin Isa Al-Khalifa, who was given the rank of minister.

The Bahraini Police Force plays a vital role in keeping peace in Bahrain.

The law courts in Bahrain conform to Islamic laws.

LEGAL STRUCTURE

Bahrain's judicial system is the responsibility of the Ministry of Justice and Islamic Affairs, under Minister of Justice, Sheikh Abdulla bin Khalid Al-Khalifa. Justice is administered under *Shariah* or Islamic law, and the judiciary is the second highest authority in Bahrain, after the personal authority of the emir. In 1997 the Directorate of Courts computerized and reorganized the legal system in the interests of making legal proceedings more accessible and efficient. The civil Court of Appeal was streamlined, new judges were appointed by decree, two new *Shariah* courts were established, and litigation was greatly facilitated. The *Shariah* courts deal primarily with personal matters such as marriage, divorce, and inheritance.

Legislative decrees and directives promulgated by the emir together with edicts and administrative circulars enacted by the prime minister are received by the Ministry of Cabinet Affairs and Information. This ministry gives them serial numbers, records them, and circulates them to government ministries, departments, and organizations.

LOCAL ADMINISTRATION

Local matters are dealt with as far as possible by the municipalities. The first to be set up was the Manama Municipality in 1926. Its president, secretary, and eight members were chosen by the ruler. The success of the municipality led to the establishment of similar bodies in other parts of Bahrain—Al-Muharraq in 1927, Hidd in 1945, then in the urban areas of Rifa, Sitrah, Jidhafs, and Isa Town, and finally in the rural regions.

Local rule has a considerable impact on the lives of citizens since the municipality is responsible for matters such as town cleaning, road building, street lights, sanitation, markets, drainage, public health, land reclamation, and the provision of water. Grants are available from the central government to cover many local activities, but decisions are made at the municipal level.

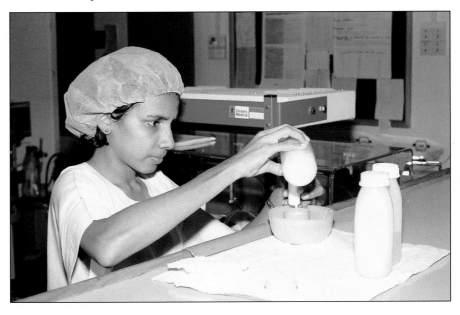

The local municipality provides healthcare services to the local population.

31

Bahrain has enjoyed peace in recent history. The only interruption was the political unrest in the mid-1990s due to demands for greater democracy.

THE POLITICAL SITUATION

The final decade of the 20th century witnessed an unusual degree of political tension in quiet Bahrain. This was dominated by relations with Iran, Bahrain's neighbor across the water, which dropped its territorial claim to Bahrain only in 1970. Internal demands for greater democracy, which took the form of protests centered in predominantly Shiite villages, culminated in riots in November 1994.

Shiite is the type of Islam followed by the majority of Bahrainis and the form of religion in Iran; it is, however, not the form adopted by the Al-Khalifas, who are Sunnis. Some of the Shiites speak Persian (Iranian) at home and sympathize with the Islamic revolution that took place in Iran. When bombs exploded at two major hotels in 1995 and 1996, the government and media of Bahrain accused Iran of inciting violence.

Following Iraq's invasion of Kuwait in 1990 and the international "Desert Storm" operation to liberate Kuwait, Bahrain's relations with Iraq rapidly deteriorated. Bahrain played a significant role in the international response to the Iraqi invasion. At the turn of the millennium, relations had improved with Iran but remained poor with Iraq.

Nearer home, the longstanding dispute with Qatar over ownership of the Hawar Islands, which Bahrain controls, shows no signs of resolution. Bahrain continues to lay claim to the Fasht al-Dibal islands and a part of mainland Qatar known as Kubara. The dispute has never resulted in hostilities and probably will not happen in the future, but so far neither side has proposed a compromise acceptable to both parties.

The new Bahrain Government House is located on Government Road in Manama. It sits on reclaimed land and overlooks the Persian Gulf.

ECONOMY

FOR THOUSAND OF YEARS Bahrain has been regarded as a paradise in a desert region. From the Stone Age through the Dilmun and Greek periods, Bahrain's natural treasures—its ports, abundant ground water, and ability to feed its people—were praised in all accounts of foreigners intent on trade with or conquest of the islands.

Surrounded by much larger countries, Bahrain has managed to avoid being swallowed up by any of them. Besides maintaining its national identity, the country has built up a thriving economy that makes it a forerunner in the Gulf region in terms of economic innovation and provision of knowledge.

Above: **Built in 1930, the Bab Al-Bahrain is one of the main tourist attractions in Bahrain.**

Opposite: **One Bahraini dinar is equivalent to 1000 fils. Dinar notes come in the denomination of 0.5, 1, 5, 10, and 20, while coins come as 5, 10, 25, 50, and 100 fils.**

SIGNIFICANT SOURCES OF REVENUE

For hundreds of years, Bahrain's principal export and most significant source of indirect revenue was pearls.

The population of Bahrain in 1905 was estimated to be 99,000. Of that number 17,500 men were divers, many of them living on Al-Muharraq. Apart from boat registration licenses, no direct taxes were levied on divers or the pearls they gathered. State revenues came from taxation of imports that were necessary to meet the new needs of a more prosperous people following the trading of pearls. Total state revenue for the year 1928/1929 was US$3.2 million of which a massive US$2.97 million was raised from pearling and customs duty.

Pearling declined in the 1930s when the world depression significantly reduced the demand for luxury goods. The growth of Japanese cultured pearls, which sold for a fraction of the price, also eclipsed the natural pearl industry of Bahrain.

PEARLING

Bahrain's pearls were famous for their clarity, brilliance, and beauty. It was believed that the finest pearls were found in oyster-beds near Bahrain's underground sweet-water springs. Most Bahraini pearlers, however, operated in various locations, many of them distant from Bahrain. This made any direct taxation problematic.

Before the 16th century, pearling involved a few men diving from mats of rushes floating in the sea. After the 16th century, between 60 and 80 men would live on board a big pearling ship throughout the pearling season, which typically lasted from June to October each year. Distant pearl-beds were well known to the pearlers of Bahrain, and during the golden age of the industry in the 1920s, more than 2,500 ships would sail from Bahrain during the pearling season.

During each pearling trip, the pearls collected were put in a common pool. At the end of the trip, they would be distributed according to the role of each participant. The captain would receive a higher share than the diver, who would in turn receive more than the cook. The singer would get the same share as each diver because of the important role he played in maintaining everyone's morale during long sea journeys. The singer was the only source of entertainment during short breaks from a very hard routine.

Pearl-beds were located at depths between 7 ba'a to 20 ba'a. One ba'a is the span of outstretched arms from finger tip to finger tip. Working at such depths was dangerous. Apart from the risks of encountering sharks, the pressure on the lungs of the divers could also lead to serious breathing problems. A good diver would dive up to 50 times a day, each time staying underwater for up to two minutes and collecting some 20 oysters from the seabed.

OIL

The decline of the pearling industry in the 1930s might have been disastrous for Bahrain if not for the foresight of the country's leader, who granted concessions to a U.S. company in 1925 to explore for oil in Bahrain. Commercial quantities of oil were discovered, and in 1932 Bahrain became the first country in the Gulf to export oil.

Oil rapidly became Bahrain's primary source of revenue. While the knowledge that oil reserves in Bahrain will be depleted by 2005 has prompted important advances in the country's education, banking, tourism, and other sectors, oil continued to generate more revenue than all other economic activities combined in the 1990s.

Bahrain's neighbors were quick to see the extraordinary wealth that flowed to Bahrain from oil. It took them some years to go through the same process of exploration, discovery, exploitation, and finally exportation. During these years, Bahrain reaped significant profits from oil and invested the money wisely. More successfully than any of its neighbors, Bahrain has made use of its oil revenues to diversify the economy, knowing that within a few years, it would move from being the biggest oil producer in the Gulf to one of the smallest.

ECONOMIC DIVERSIFICATION

To diversify its economy, Bahrain has welcomed foreign investors. Large shipbuilding and repair yards service the world's traders today. Bahrain International Airport, one of the region's biggest airports, has been named the best, busiest, and cheapest stop in the world.

The banking and tourism sectors have grown quickly, and their development shows no sign of stopping in the near future. The opening of the King Fahd Causeway between Bahrain and Saudi Arabia in 1986 was an added boost for business and tourism. Bahrain and its people have demonstrated an ability to embrace change, leading to the prosperity of this small island-state.

The wharf at Sitrah provides repair and maintenance services to international ships.

ALUMINUM

In 1968 Bahrain began a concerted program of economic diversification. The government played an active role in the establishment of big-scale industries, one of them being the large-scale aluminum smelting project. This has matured to become the backbone of the country's industrial development. Today Aluminum Bahrain (ALBA), a joint venture between Bahrain and Saudi Arabia, is the Middle East's largest and one of the world's top three producers of aluminum and aluminum alloys. Based on ALBA's annual output of half a million tons, many related industries have been established, which include a rolling mill, automobile wheel factories, and an extrusion plant.

Heavy machinery is used to stack the molded aluminum before it is exported.

Besides the big players in oil and aluminum, there are many small to medium-sized companies, such as the above spring mattress factory.

MANUFACTURING

Bahrain has succeeded in attracting industry by offering foreign investors a tax-free environment, a currency tied to the U.S. dollar, low inflation, no restriction on movement of funds, no personal taxation and, unique among the Gulf Cooperation Council (GCC) countries, 100% foreign ownership, which means no local partner is required. This translates into lower costs for manufacturing and services compared with Europe and North America.

Bahrain also offers the best standard of education and training in the region. Skilled labor can be hired at around US$400 per month, much less than in other Arab countries. The widespread usage of English is another factor acting in Bahrain's favor.

Bahrain's well-established infrastructure ensures that business will operate smoothly according to international commercial law. The country is a founding member of the World Trade Organization and at the forefront of discussions related to updating regulations to cope with advances in technology and commerce. An excellent banking system provides essential support. The land link with Saudi Arabia provides direct access to a market of 24 million people with high disposable incomes.

The trump card for Bahrain is perhaps the low cost of overhead. Office rental in Manama's business district is among the lowest of the world's capitals, and utilities are provided at very low rates.

Within a short time the manufacturing industry has increased to the point where it now provides revenues equal to the oil and gas industries, contributing 18% of the gross domestic product (GDP).

BANKING

In 1975 Bahrain established financial regulations governing offshore banking, paving the way for international commercial, investment, and offshore banks to operate freely. It remains the only country in the region to allow such institutions. Today financial institutions contribute about 17% to Bahrain's GDP.

Not only is Bahrain a regional center for banking and finance, it has also earned a world reputation for economic freedom, ranking third consistently in the world after Hong Kong and Singapore on the American Heritage Foundation's Index of Economic Freedom.

The first of the 12 top Islamic banks in Bahrain opened in 1983. Such banks enjoy favorable public support from Islamic investors and savers. These banks essentially target the Middle East, the most significant source of funds for religiously ethical investments.

Islamic banks are managed in accordance with the *Shariah* which prohibits the lending of money at exorbitant rates of interest.

Windsurfing is one of the water sports available at the Meridien Hotel.

TOURISM

Today tourism contributes 11% to the nation's gross domestic product and attracts approximately 2.5 million visitors a year. As Bahrain enters the new millennium, it is placing more emphasis on its already well-established tourism sector.

Compared to countries outside the Middle East, Bahrain is conservative. Compared to its neighbors, the country is positively liberal. This is the principal attraction for the many tourists, three quarters of whom cross the causeway from Saudi Arabia. The total number of tourist arrivals has grown by 18% since 1986.

Visitors, usually Arabs and expatriates working in other countries in the region, come for a variety of reasons. For these tourists, Bahrain is a nearby location for a weekend break. Its comparative liberalism allows women, usually foreigners, to wear swimming suits in appropriate areas. Alcohol is also available in expensive hotel bars and night clubs, in principle only for non-Muslims.

DEVELOPMENT FOR THE FUTURE

Bahrain is capitalizing on its unique geographic location and has started the construction of a new 2.5-square-mile (6.5-square-km) industrial and duty-free zone. This new development at Hidd, near Al-Hadd, is a 15-minute drive from Bahrain International Airport and will have a port three times the capacity of the existing facility at Mina Salman. It will also have a direct road connection with the King Fahd Causeway to Saudi Arabia to facilitate shopping trips from the mainland.

Bahrain plans to continue its strong commitment to what is frequently called the country's most valuable natural resource—the Bahraini people. In 1998, for the third consecutive year, the United Nations Development Program (UNDP), taking into account health services, education, life expectancy, and per capita income, ranked Bahrain as the number one country in the Arab world for human development.

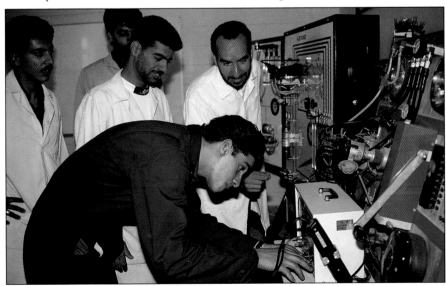

Bahrain is counting on its people to continue the nation's prosperity in the new millennium as natural resources such as oil become depleted.

BAHRAINIS

BAHRAIN IS THE ONLY ARAB ISLAND-STATE in the Persian Gulf. Its Arabness is evident in the people, the national language, and the state religion. Many Bahrainis have a mixed ancestry resulting from the long period of Persian rule. They practice Shiite Islam and speak Farsi (Persian) at home. Almost all Bahrainis working in trade, banking, and industry use English as the language of commerce.

Most Bahrainis are Muslims, and about 60% of them practice the Shiite school of Islam, which came from Iran. The remaining Bahraini Muslims adhere to the more universally accepted Sunni interpretation. Of the two branches of Islam, neither can claim to be more Bahraini than the other.

Bahrain converted to Islam during Prophet Mohammed's lifetime, when Sunni and Shiite divisions did not exist. The population for several thousand years before that point was racially comparable to that of the

Left: **A mother supervising her sons' homework. Bahrainis spend a lot of time with their families, both in and outside of the home.**

Opposite: **Few weavers remain today in the small village of Bani Jamrah, which once boasted of a thousand weavers who produced cloth for traditional Bahraini clothing.**

45

In public, Bahrainis are likely to converse in Arabic, the official and most commonly used language in Bahrain.

Arabian mainland, where the first Bahrainis probably came from during the Stone Age. Culturally Bahrainis evolved more in line with Mesopotamia, which also influenced people in the coastal region of the Arabian Gulf.

Throughout a long history as a trading nation, there have been many traders from other lands who have remained in Bahrain, where the grass was literally greener. Over the years population changes and movements have been gradual and regional, with the exception of a small minority of Greeks, Indians, and a few Africans. The evolutionary result is a Bahraini identity and culture which is not as homogeneously Arab as the peoples of Saudi Arabia. The great majority of citizens think of themselves as Arabs and as Bahrainis. To distinguish them from the Arabs of Saudi Arabia, Egypt, and beyond, Bahraini Arabs, along with Arabs from Kuwait, Qatar, Oman, and the United Arab Emirates, are often referred to as Gulf Arabs.

THE ARABS

Led by the Al-Khalifa family clan, the tribes that settled in Bahrain after conquering the Persian rulers were Arabs in the fullest sense. The confederation of tribes known as Utoob also took control of much of the maritime Gulf as far north as Kuwait.

It is believed that the Utoob, driven by hunger, migrated from the desert regions of Saudi Arabia at the end of the 17th century, splitting up when they reached the shores of the Arabian Gulf. The first group arrived in Bahrain in 1701. Following several takeover attempts, the Al-Khalifas established their rule over Bahrain and have since maintained purity of line and remained fully Arab in every sense.

In the past, unfavorable climate forced tribes from Saudi Arabia to cross the desert in search of greener pastures.

GUEST WORKERS

Bahrain is the only country in the Gulf where the population of citizens exceeds guest workers. Today there are about 401,289 Bahrainis compared to 227, 801 non-Bahrainis. Although citizens make up about 64% of Bahrain's population, there are more non-Bahrainis than Bahrainis in the labor force. Bahrainis account for only about 38% of the work force, while non-Bahrainis constitute the remaining 62%.

Skilled and unskilled guest workers poured into Bahrain in the 1930s when oil first was discovered. Many guest workers became rich overnight, and the prospect of instant wealth attracted more people. To prevent new migrants from swamping the country and its culture, these workers were mostly given short-term contracts and rotated among other Middle East countries, who faced the same problems.

By 1941 there were four or five non-Bahrainis in the country to every Bahraini citizen. This situation lasted until 1971, when the government made a concerted effort to reduce the proportion of foreigners. Although not all foreign workers work in oil-related industry, the revenue from oil makes it possible to pay them a wage significantly higher than what they could hope to earn in their home countries.

BAHRAINI DRESS

The costumes of Bahrainis are essentially the same as those seen in Arabia and elsewhere in the Gulf. Bahrainis wear their national dress on a daily basis, although the finest clothes are kept for special occasions. It is common to see Bahraini children dressed in T-shirts and shorts. However, the older generation still prefers traditional dress.

Conservative Western suits are occasionally worn in offices. Foreigners, though not expected to adhere to Bahraini dress codes, are required to dress modestly. Guest workers are easily distinguishable from Arabs (not necessarily Bahrainis) because of their Western-style attire.

Left: **Children are allowed to wear Western casual outfits, but adults have to wear the national dress every day.**

Opposite: **Foreign workers making *dhows* ("DOWS"). Foreign workers are mostly employed to fill positions which require less skill.**

On special occasions such as festivals and weddings, Bahraini women will dress themselves in exquisite and elaborate costumes.

A BAHRAINI LADY'S WARDROBE

The Bahraini lady's *thaub* ("THAR-oob") is made by joining rectangular pieces of light materials like cotton or silk into a large square with a hole in the middle. It goes over the head, rests on the shoulders, and flows down to the ground. Several types of *thaub* exist, and the name of each indicates the material and the kind of embroidery used.

The most exquisite *thaubs* are used to dress a bride and to celebrate special occasions and festivals. Made of red, green, or purple silk, always of a single color, they are decorated with elaborate, usually gold, embroidery.

When stepping outdoors, the Bahraini lady will wear a *daffa* ("DAH-fah"), a long garment that covers the head and opens at the front. It is intricately embroidered with golden silk and may be decorated with gold jewels. Alternatively she may wear a *milfa* ("MILL-fah"), a black, rectangular piece of net-like cotton on her head and that lowers to cover her face.

Underneath it all, the Bahraini lady wears a *dara'a* ("DAH-rah"), a long loose underdress which may also be embroidered at the cuffs. On her feet, she wears either leather or wooden sandals.

THE EXPOSURE FACTOR

The Koran stipulates that women must be clothed from head to toe, although variance to this rule is possible. In some societies, "head to toe" is taken literally, and women only appear in public wrapped in a huge piece of cloth, usually black with little decoration, which goes over the head and flows to the ground. The cloth is thin enough for the woman to see through, yet thick enough to prevent the world from looking in.

The face mask or veil is used in some Muslim countries, both of which cover the entire face except for the eyes. In other countries, women cover half the face, leaving one eye and half a mouth to guide them through the public.

Bahrain is considered the most liberal among the Middle Eastern countries. A woman's face and hands may be fully in view. Female workers may wear uniforms or follow a conservative dress code that is not necessarily based on Arabic clothing. Schoolgirls also wear uniforms which closely resemble those of their English counterparts. They do not have to wear veils to cover their heads. The dress code in the capital of Manama is more liberal than in the surrounding suburbs and distant villages.

Bahraini men wear light cotton clothes, which are usually white to reflect the heat of the sun.

MALE COSTUME

During summer, men may wear light clothes, which consist of a headdress, a white summer robe, both usually cotton, and open sandals. In winter, heavier, woolen clothes and an undershirt that reaches to the ankles are worn.

The cotton garment has long, white sleeves and no collar, with a tassel attached to the neck opening. It is made of vertical rectangular pieces except for the sleeves which are triangular. There is usually pale silk embroidery around the neck opening.

As a contrast to the simple, white robe, the head cloth Bahraini men wear may be checkered or embroidered. It is kept in place by a twisted white or black cord. The wealthier Bahrainis may be seen in clothes made of the finest wool or silk.

The man's cloak is a sign of prestige and status. It is similar to a woman's cloak, except that it is usually made of camel hair and has less embroidery.

The handmade sandals worn by men may be locally made or imported from India, Saudi Arabia, or Iraq. The plain leather open sandal with a partition for the big toe is most commonly seen, but sandals elaborately decorated in gold and silver are also popular.

Children in their school uniforms assembling in front of the school before class begins.

CHILDREN'S DRESS

Clothing for children is a miniature version of what their parents wear and reflects the status of the parents. Young children may be seen wearing imported brand name Western clothing, such as T-shirts and jeans.

Most schoolchildren wear Western-style uniforms although some of the more conservative schools still require their students to wear traditional Arabic-style uniforms.

CLEANLINESS

Cleanliness and modesty are the two guiding principles of Bahraini dress, as they are of the Bahraini lifestyle.

Bahrainis, many of whom have no need to go out to work, spend much time and money on their clothes. They also bathe and put on clean clothes frequently.

Bahrain can only be considered liberal when compared to other Gulf states. By Western standards, it is very conservative. There are taboos against short skirts, shorts, tight tops, and unnecessary exposure of the body. Men are not allowed to walk around bare-chested.

Much of the underlying rationale for dress and cleanliness is written in the Koran, which states that cleanliness is next to Godliness.

LIFESTYLE

THE ESSENCE OF BAHRAIN'S HERITAGE can be found in the lives of its people, their customs, traditions, dress, education, health, and housing style, as well as in the way they go about their daily lives. Passed down through generations, the Bahraini culture is reinforced by Islamic principles and examples set or dictated by the elders. Every stage of a Bahraini's life involves traditions and ceremonies of some kind, and the guiding hands of religion and the older and wiser generation are always present.

LIFECYCLE EVENTS

While change is apparent in Bahrain, the basic rhythms of life in the rural parts of the country remain largely traditional. Traditions in Bahraini society are very much alive, and these are seen in the rituals performed during the significant points of the lifecycle—birth, marriage, and death.

Left: **A group of Bahrainis gathered to play a word game.**

Opposite: **In wealthy Bahrain the elderly enjoy a relaxed lifestyle, spending their time with family or friends. Many of them seek pleasure from smoking hubble-bubble pipes.**

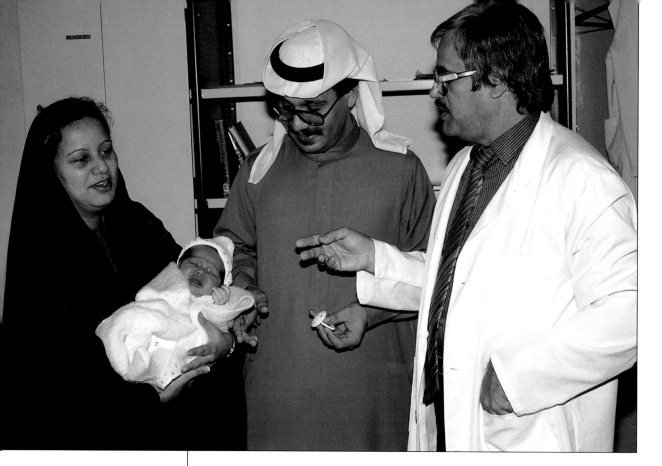

BIRTH

Less than 3% of births take place in the home today because Bahrainis are aware that a baby's chance of survival is the highest in a hospital, where professional help and adequate facilities are readily available. They do not, however, abandon traditional practices, even if these have to take place in the hospital.

Before entering a hospital to give birth, a Bahraini woman, set on honoring her parents and preparing herself for the birth, will return to her father's house, where herbs and nourishing food are prepared for her. In the past her delivery would have been assisted by her mother, sisters, and a professional midwife, and traditional rituals were performed at home.

Today the customary ritual cup of water and three dried dates are likely to be brought to the hospital by the mother. The newborn is rubbed with herbs, wrapped in soft, fresh, cotton cloth, and placed in a cradle. To introduce the baby to Islam, the all-important call to prayer is recited in the baby's right ear, and the prayer is recited in his left ear.

CIRCUMCISION

According to Arabic tradition, Muslim boys are to have their foreskins removed. This takes place between the ages of three and six, usually in the spring, with favorite days being Monday, Thursday, and Friday, or a religious occasion such as the Prophet's Birthday. Today circumcision is more likely to be done in a clinic under sterile conditions. For the previous generation, the operation was performed in the house, and herbal medicine would be applied to the wound. Sea bathing would also be ordered to clean it. Whatever the changes, the essence of this ancient tradition continues. Circumcision is thought to make a boy a full member of the Islamic community and is cause for celebration.

When the woman returns home with the baby, a small family feast will be prepared, and a chicken slaughtered. In the past the umbilical cord was buried, next to the mosque if the baby was a boy, and in the kitchen if it was a girl. Few Bahrainis would dig up their kitchen floor for this purpose today, especially if they live in an air-conditioned apartment.

The baby is usually named on the second day after birth. This name almost always follows a tradition that emphasizes the importance of continuity between generations of a family in the male line—the baby boy receives his grandfather's name or another name in remembered lineage, while the baby girl receives her grandmother's name.

Traditionally the mother and child remained in the mother's parental home for 40 days after the birth to allow the new mother to recover her strength. During this period, many of the daily tasks would be done for her by her mother and sisters. After these 40 days, the mother and baby returned to the husband's home together with the mother's female relatives. The husband would receive and thank them and give a present to his wife and baby as a welcome gesture.

A child's firsts are deemed significant. In the past the first haircut involved carefully collecting the hair and weighing it on a small set of scales using coins as counterweights. These coins would then be distributed to other children. The first tooth and first steps were traditionally celebrated, and a basket of sweets, nuts, and coins was thrown over the head of the child to other older children. These customs are still practiced today in an abridged form.

A bride in traditional wedding dress. A typical Bahraini wedding is characterized by lavish costumes, music, and a feast.

MARRIAGE

Modernization has hardly changed marriage. Love matches play no part at all, and no Bahraini girl could hope to get away with rejecting the husband her parents have chosen for her. Some families will consult their children as to their preferences, but the real decision lies with the fathers of the bride and groom.

Bahrainis, like most Arabic people, believe the ideal union is that between what anthropologists call patrilateral parallel cousins. In other words, it is a marriage between a man and his father's brother's daughter, or, looking at things from the bride's point of view, between a woman and her father's brother's son. This preference predates the advent of Islam and was once found in many ancient societies such as Greece and China. This is often done to ensure that property and rank is retained within a single male line of descent. In Bahraini society the greater a family's property, the more likely this form of marriage is to occur. With each such union, the strong bond between brothers is reinforced, as is the alliance between more distant members of the extended family. This traditional preference for marriage partners explains the centuries of rule by the Al-Khalifa family.

The traditional preference is not obligatory, and sometimes, it cannot be considered because the groom's father's brothers have no female children of a suitable age. Under such circumstances, it is time to contact an *al-khataba* ("al-KAH-tah-bah"), a matchmaker, usually female, to look for a wife.

The search for a marriage partner is always initiated by the groom's side, never by the bride or her family. The most common practice is to engage an *al-khataba* who has no links to either the groom's family or any of the families under review. Discreet enquiries may be made without any obligation and, of paramount importance, with no loss of face for anyone if an enquiry is not followed up.

A Bahraini selecting a gift for his intended wife. Popular gifts include gold jewelry such as a necklace, bracelet, or ring.

The *al-khataba* is informed of the groom's and his family's personal circumstances and preferences. If interest is shown, the *al-khataba* undertakes an intensive investigation of the girl's background and the circumstances and behavior of the members of her family. She then reports back to the groom's family, who will look at the girl's reputation, demeanor, and ability to manage household chores.

If both families are happy with the reports from the *al-Khataba*, the female members of the two families may meet for the first time to confirm their support for the match. Only when the fathers of both the groom and the bride have agreed to the match will the marriage become assured. Male members of both families will discuss the *dazeh* ("DAH-zeh") or bride price to be paid and set a date for the wedding.

HERE COMES THE BAHRAINI BRIDE

A few days before the wedding, a good luck party is held for the bride. At this all-female occasion, the bride sits on a chair holding a basket of sweets, while women recite religious verses. Four women hold a green cloth above the head of the bride and lift it up and down while singing. This is to wish the bride well in her marriage.

The night before the wedding day, a henna night is held for the bride. At this pre-wedding ceremony, a special designer will paint the bride's hands and feet with intricate patterns using henna, a natural dye. Meanwhile the guests sing and play drums. The bride must be careful not to be seen by the guests, or it is believed that her face will lose its beauty.

On the wedding day the bride is dressed in a plain silk *thaub*. No jewelry is worn. An expert hairdresser is hired to prepare the bride's hair and adorn it with basil and jasmine. The groom's mother goes with her female relatives and neighbors to the bride's house to present the *dazeh*. At the house of the bride, the largest room will be elaborately decorated. Relatives and neighbors will lend mirrors, carpets, and seating cushions to accommodate the many guests.

At night, the groom and his relatives receive guests in his house before leaving for the house of the bride's father. On arrival the groom is shown to the prepared wedding room to await the bride. Dressed in a plain silk *thaub* and a white *daffa,* she is brought to him sitting on a carpet carried

by four women. The bridal pair are left alone. A group of musicians play loudly outside the wedding room while the marriage is consummated.

The next day a feast is held. Food is served in the wedding room for male relatives and friends of the groom. The bride is not present during this feast. On the same day the groom gives his wife a piece of "binding" jewelry, such as a necklace, bracelet, or ring, so that she will not leave him.

Only on the third day after the wedding can the bride's guests visit and congratulate her. The bride receives them in her finest clothes and literally dripping in gold. She must appear prosperous for the sake of her husband's pride.

OLD AGE AND DEATH

Both parents and grandparents are greatly respected in a Bahraini family, and in old age, they will be well cared for by their children. The oldest male in the Bahraini family has the most authority in the household and is the principal decision-maker. The oldest woman's power extends only as far as her influence over her husband or, if the husband is dead, over her eldest son.

When death comes, relatives and neighbors are contacted immediately, and nearly all of them will visit the family to pay their respects to the departed and console the family. Burial is the accepted practice and is usually performed before the next day's sunset, in accordance with the Koran. The body is wrapped in a sheet and buried in a grave with only a simple marker since the deceased is assumed to be in paradise and needs no elaborate material reminders of his or her time on earth.

Elderly Bahraini men enjoying a smoke. Bahrainis 65 years old and above make up 2% of the population.

A family enjoying a feast. The Bahraini lifestyle revolves around the family.

THE FAMILY

The typical Bahraini family extends to at least three generations. It is the foundation of Bahraini life and the frame of reference of any member's social and legal identity. As an institution, it is intrinsically tied to the code of conduct involved in maintaining face. Family honor depends on the mutual solidarity of its members and adherence to the basic codes of behavior—respect, modesty, obedience, and generosity. The formation of marital alliances between family groups creates a larger mutual commitment to honor and generosity. Proper conduct between relatives relies on a full understanding of the rights and duties pertaining to any one member of the family, from the young child to the old grandparent or great-grandparent.

Traditionally the three generations would all live under the same roof—father and mother, their unmarried children, their married sons with their wives and children, a divorced or widowed daughter, sister, or mother. Daughters would leave the home when married and live in the house of

FACE AND FAMILY

Face is everything to the Bahrainis. Children learn about it from an early age—if a neighbor breaks the law or one of the invisible rules that keep society together, that is, the social rules of respect, modesty, obedience, and hospitality—the neighbor's children will find few playmates. The Bahraini child grows up in a social environment where respect for elders and family honor are taught; to conform to the pattern brings praise; to rebel, even mildly, brings some form of punishment or admonition. Physical punishment is not unknown, but it is unnecessary for most families. A gentle, friendly reproof, coupled with a warning, is almost always enough to bring a child into line. A firmer measure would be a temporary banishment to the bedroom, i.e. away from the rest of the family. Although it is largely symbolic, this gives the child time to reflect on how puny he or she is without the strength and comfort of the family.

A child quickly comes to realize that face and honor, on which he or she will be judged by society at large throughout life, is bound to that of the family. Behavior of a doubtful nature by a relative, even a quite distant one, threatens the honor of the family, which takes centuries to build up, and one thoughtless action of a deviant family member could destroy it altogether. In the modern world wealth increases face, and so does education. It is, however, not enough to compensate for breach of etiquette, and by extension, to fail in business or to fail examinations constitutes a loss of face for the individual and his or her family.

their husband's father. Today the demands of city life have caused some changes in residential patterns. It is now acceptable that after a few years in his father's house, a man with growing sons of his own may take them and their mother and move to an apartment near his place of work. There is, however, at least one son and his nuclear family who will remain in the parental home. Compared to other countries, nuclear families are not as widespread in Bahrain because many men do not work and their family homes are large and conveniently located.

Children are loved by their parents and are included in all Bahraini social activity. Small children, including girls, are welcome in adult male gatherings in the household. As they grow, children are separated by gender long before puberty; boys may accompany their fathers, while older daughters are expected to remain in the home with their mother.

Bahraini society remains essentially home-based. Few social activities are restricted to adults. Parents constantly interact with their children. Home-centered social life involves socializing with relatives and neighbors while respecting the strict line separating sexes.

Older children of the wealthier Bahraini families may be sent to the United Kingdom for further education, but generally children do not expect and are not expected to spend nights away from home.

EDUCATION

Largely due to its small population, Bahrain has long seen education of its people as necessary if the island is to survive and prosper. Today the country has some of the best schools in the region, and a significant number of students go on to study at the University of Bahrain, the Arabian Gulf University, or overseas, most in the United States or the United Kingdom. The teaching staff in Bahrain are almost entirely Bahraini.

The government extends free education to all and goes to great lengths to ensure that girls are given equal opportunities in education. In 1997 there were 182 government-financed schools, 92 of which were for boys and the rest reserved for girls. The literacy rate is high enough for the population to be considered fully literate. Adult education centers are available to provide courses to adults who missed out or needed to revise their skills to meet the demands of changing job markets.

Bahrain has led the Arab world in embracing modern education, extending education to women, and building a diverse vocational environment on a firm base of education. Many non-Bahraini companies in the region, wanting to take advantage of skilled trainers and sophisticated equipment, send their staff to Bahrain for training.

As in most countries of the world, the first schools were religious in nature and had the goal of teaching the scriptures and creating good citizens. In Bahrain before 1919, the only schools were Koranic schools, where boys and girls were taught classical Arabic pronunciation and grammar, along with the meaning and significance of the texts.

In the early years of the 20th century the American Mission School opened its doors to Bahraini children. Bahrain's first Minister of Education, Sheikh Abdullah bin Isa Al-Khalifa, formed an education committee in 1919 and opened the first modern Bahraini school for boys, the al-Hidaya Al-Khalifaya School in Al-Muharraq.

Bahraini women learning to use computers.

The first girls' school started nine years later in Al-Muharraq. It was so popular that another school opened in Manama a year later. The curriculum was similar to that in the boys' school, with the addition of domestic hygiene, cooking, dressmaking, and embroidery. After 1931, education became the direct concern of the government. By 1956, the year in which Saudi Arabia set up its first school for girls, Bahrain had 3,953 girls attending 13 schools with 103 teachers, of whom 94 were Bahrainis.

The schools in Bahrain are divided by gender and their amenities compare very well with any school in the world. Uniforms, which are not based on traditional clothing, are worn, and female students are not required to cover their heads.

HEALTH

Bahrain has invested the revenue from oil in its most valuable resource, its people, improving educational facilities and health services greatly since the 1940s.

The first state hospital was opened in stages from 1939 to 1942 at Naim. This was followed by the Salmaniya Hospital in 1959. At the end of the 20th century, there were four government hospitals in Bahrain with a total of 1,540 beds and three private hospitals with 177 beds. The ratio of hospital beds to patients is 1:3, and the ratio of doctors to patients is 1:9. With basic vaccination of the entire population hitting 95% in 1997, Bahrain's health service is ranked among the best in the world.

Right: **Largely due to better heathcare, the life expectancy of Bahrainis has increased from 65 years in the 1980s to the present 75 years.**

Opposite: **A local medicine and herb seller in Manama. The widespread use of Western medicine in Bahrain has not eliminated the use of traditional herbs as an alternative curative measure.**

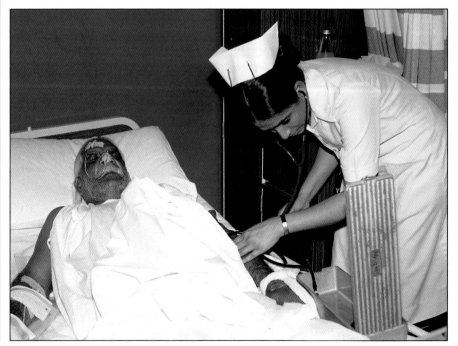

Bahrain remains dependent on foreigners for its medical staff. In 1997, 57% of all doctors were Bahraini, 90% of all dentists were Bahraini citizens, and so were 43% of the nurses. The government is committed to Bahrainization in health services, and these percentages are expected to change rapidly as more Bahraini women enter the work force after completing higher education and specialist training.

Prior to the discovery and export of oil in 1932, state medical services were basic and inadequate. There were little more than a few small dispensaries and a quarantine service.

The two hospitals set up and run by foreign charities could do little for the general population. With very limited access to modern medicine, most of the population relied on traditional medicine which was a mixture of herbalism and magic. Herbs were readily available for purchase from a herb seller who possessed a knowledge of the curative properties of indigenous and imported plants compiled over the centuries. Such alternative medicine is still in use in modern Bahrain. On the other hand, magical remedies and protections, which usually involve wearing amulets containing Koranic verses or the repetition of the Koran over a sick person, inspire little confidence today.

RELIGION

EIGHTY-FIVE PER CENT OF BAHRAINI CITIZENS adhere to the state religion of Islam. The remaining 15% are indigenous Bahrainis who follow Christian, Jewish, Hindu, or Parsee faiths.

THE PRINCIPLES OF ISLAM

The word Islam means submission, or more precisely, submission to the will of God. Muslims, followers of Islam, believe there is only one God, Allah, who created and sustains the world and everything in it.

Muslims believe that Mohammed was the last and greatest of a series of God's prophets, which included Jesus Christ. Mohammed received messages from God when he was in a trance, and his disciples collected these messages, revealed through Mohammed over the course of 20 years, and compiled them into the Koran ("KOH-ran").

The exact wording of the Koran, as it is read today, was set down by disciples and scholars after Mohammed's death in A.D. 632. The success of their work, in classical Arabic, is evident in the great number of non-Muslims who, after reading it, consider the Koran the religious and literary masterpiece of all time. The Koran has been translated into every major language of the world, but all over the world Muslims learn the original Arabic text.

In addition to the Koran, the word of God, Muslims follow the *Hadith* ("ha-DEETH"), a record of the Prophet's sayings. These offer detailed guidance for daily life from how to wash to how to forgive other people.

Above: **An old restored Koran.**

Opposite: **The Al-Fatih Mosque is the largest building in Bahrain and can accommodate 7,000 worshippers.**

Because Bahrain is located near Mecca and most Bahrainis are wealthy and can afford to pay the expenses, almost all Bahraini Muslims make the pilgrimage to Mecca each year.

THE FIVE PILLARS OF ISLAM

Following Mohammed's death, his followers formalized five key responsibilities or actions that Muslims should try to fulfill. Known as the five pillars of Islam, these actions apply equally to men and women.

1. SHAHADAH ("sha-HAHD-ah") Muslims must declare in Arabic, "There is no God other than God; Mohammed is the Messenger of God." Reciting this statement is all that is needed to convert to Islam from another religion.

2. SALAT ("sa-LAHT") means prayer. Muslims should pray five times daily—before sunrise, in the early afternoon, late afternoon, after sunset, and before going to bed. Prayers may be offered anywhere. Women usually pray at home with other women. Office workers will have a room set aside where they can pray with their colleagues. Few Bahrainis go to the mosque for every prayer session, but all will try to attend Friday prayers, when the *imam* ("ee-MAHM"), the prayer leader, reads a text from the Koran and gives a sermon.

3. ZAKAT ("zah-KART") is alms-giving. Muslims should pay the *zakat* or religious tax to help the poor.

4. SAWM ("sa-AHM") means fasting. Muslims should fast from dawn to dusk everyday during the holy month of Ramadan. Fasting is defined as no eating, no liquids, no smoking, and no sexual activity.

5. HAJJ ("HAHJ") Muslims should make at least one pilgrimage or *hajj* to Mecca, the birthplace of Mohammed, if they can afford it. Each year at a time set according to the Islamic calendar, up to 2 million Muslims from all over the world converge in Mecca to walk seven times around the Ka'bah, a huge, sacred black stone, drink from the well of Zamzam, walk between two low hills, have their heads shaved, stand on the plain of Arafat, cast stones at the devil while calling out "Allahu Akbar" (God is Great), and pay for the sacrifice of a sheep to give to the poor.

Since cleanliness is a major concern when performing the actions associated with the pillars, women may not pray or fast when they are menstruating. The sick are also excused from fasting. All who do not fast for various reasons should keep a note of the number of days missed and add them on at the end of the fasting month or when circumstances allow.

Below: **Millions of Muslims from around the world gather at Mecca, the birthplace of Mohammed, every year.**

PROPHET MOHAMMED

Prophet Mohammed was born poor in A.D. 570. He was orphaned when very young. When he was older, he worked as a trader and married Khadijah, his first wife, when he was 25 and she was 40. Khadijah was a wealthy widow, and they had a daughter, Fatima. Mohammed remarried after the death of Khadijah. Although he became wealthy, the prophet led a simple life, helping many people who crossed his path.

Prophet Mohammed's religious ideas were initially opposed, forcing him to flee from Mecca to Medina in A.D. 622. The Islamic calendar dates from the day of this journey. In Medina Prophet Mohammed founded the first Muslim community.

He returned to Mecca with armed supporters a few years later and died in A.D. 632.

The life of Prophet Mohammed, as recorded in writing by his followers, provides a guide to Muslims on how to live the perfect life. Muslims do not worship Mohammed, but they consider acts to be good if Mohammed did them. In reality, not everyone can do what he did.

SHIITE AND SUNNI MUSLIMS

In Bahrain the ruling family is Sunni, as are most Arabs. Among Arab states, Bahrain is exceptional because about 65% of its population follows the Shiite school of Islam. Both branches maintain the basic principles and the five pillars of Islam, and while people tend to marry within their own religious grouping, there is no prohibition on intermarriage. Although all Bahraini Shiites can speak Arabic, many continue to use Farsi, the language of Persia, at home. There is no obvious antipathy between Sunni and Shiite, but the two communities have a strong inclination to live apart in exclusive neighborhoods, each with its own mosques.

The Koran House, or Beit Al-Quran, is a museum and research center in Manama that is home to a large collection of Korans, some dating from the seventh century.

Shiites constitute a greater proportion of the village-based population than is relative to their representation in the total population, and Sunnis dominate the authority structure. Various demands and actions related to a movement for increased popular democracy stem from the Shiite community. There is a division between the Sunnis and Shiites, but it has nothing to do with the differences between the two Islamic schools of thought and should not be overemphasized. The Bahraini identity is strong enough to contain both of them.

The origin of differences can be traced back to the death of Prophet Mohammed. The prophet died leaving no adult sons, and this led to some conflict over who should succeed him. Abu Bakr, a close friend of Mohammed, was chosen to lead the Muslim community. The Shiites broke away from the majority view and decided on Ali, the prophet's son-in-law, to lead them. Having deviated from the main body of Islamic thought, Shiites evolved a somewhat different interpretation of Islamic teachings, introduced their own calendar, and celebrated events related to the lives of those people they believe should have inherited the leadership mantle.

Before entering a mosque, everyone must remove his shoes and wash his feet. Visitors must be modestly dressed, with their arms and legs covered and a headcovering worn.

THE MOSQUE

The world's first two mosques, the Quba Mosque, and the Prophet's Mosque were both built in Medina under the direction of Prophet Mohammed. These two mosques set out the basic features for all mosques—a mosque must be clean, provide water for washing and, most important, it must be built so that the congregation faces Mecca in prayer. The domes and the distinctive minaret, from which the faithful are called to prayer five times a day, were added to mosque architecture only later.

The pious habit of replacing an old mosque with a new one means that there are few old mosques remaining in Bahrain. The oldest mosque is the Al-Khamis Mosque, which was founded around A.D. 720, although all that remains from the original building is the Quibla wall. In 1058 the mosque was restored by two prominent Bahrainis. A simple rectangular structure, which remains visible below the present mosque, was built in the 12th century and enlarged several times between the 14th and 16th centuries.

The mosque has a special place in Muslim community life. For many older Bahrainis, it is the place they learned to read and write. Many of them began their studies at the Grand Mosque

(Al-Jamea), which is a center of Islamic education for all ages and levels. Young children today continue the tradition of Koranic school, usually in or next to the mosque.

As a place of worship, the mosque is quite different from a church. There are no priests in Islam, and any man may teach or lead a congregation of faithful followers in prayer. In practice, however, the community employs an *imam*, somebody known for his standing in the community and vast religious knowledge. He oversees the maintenance of the mosque and organizes activities associated with the mosque community, particularly during the month of Ramadan.

While mosques are an established part of the Bahrain landscape, they are not essential to prayer, which may take place anywhere. The mosque is essentially a community building. Muslims believe that it is better to pray in the company of others—whether in a mosque, or in a room set aside in an office or other place of work—with water available to wash before prayer.

Above: **The Grand Mosque has libraries, offices for judges and administrators, as well as rooms for students in need of a place to study.**

Opposite: **Built in A.D. 720, the Al-Khamis Mosque is one of the oldest mosques in Bahrain.**

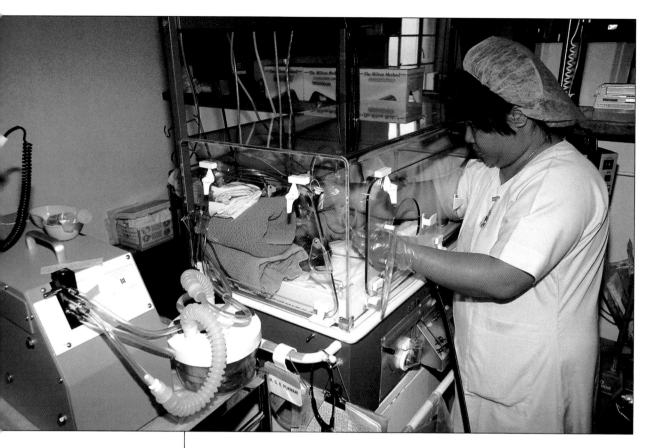

NON-MUSLIMS

Bahrain has a small Christian community, the result of missionary activity in the early 20th century. Other small, non-Muslim communities include Jewish, Hindu, and Parsee. The Jews may be descendants of the original population that did not convert to Islam when invited to do so by Prophet Mohammed. The Hindus and the Parsees came to Bahrain long ago as traders and later settled there.

All non-Muslims, about 15% of the population, are free to practice their religion. Missionary activity, however, is banned, and any conversion away from Islam is not recognized. Muslims are permitted to marry non-Muslims if the non-Muslim converts to Islam. These converts are welcomed by everyone in the Muslim community. This one-way conversion suggests that non-Muslim communities will slowly dwindle.

TRADITIONAL PRACTICES

Prophet Mohammed denounced superstition, idol worship, and any form of magic. Good Muslims though they are, Bahrainis still admit to being influenced by superstition and have a mild belief in magical powers, very often linked to Islam. They believe that Koranic verses, either written on charms and amulets or used in jewelry and house decorations, can bring good luck and remove any evil forces. For example, some people are said to possess the power of the evil eye. One glance from such a person is enough to make nasty things happen unless corrective action is taken. In this case, water that runs over a gold plate on which Koranic verses are written may be drunk by the victim as a curative measure.

For good luck, some Bahrainis wear necklaces with little casings for holding excerpts of the Koran.

LANGUAGE

ARABIC IS THE NATIONAL LANGUAGE of Bahrain and is spoken by every citizen. Bahrainis, who speak Farsi at home and Arabic in public, recognize Arabic as the sacred language of all Muslims. Guest workers generally do not speak Arabic, but many are able to get by in English, which is the language of commerce, industry, and technical education in Bahrain. Almost all educated Bahrainis speak good English.

ARABIC

Arabic is a Semitic language related to Hebrew and Aramaic. It is one of the official languages recognized by the United Nations and the official language of 17 countries. Arabic is spoken by about 200 million people from Morocco to the Middle East and the Arabian peninsula. Many non-Arabic Muslims have also learned to read the Koran and have at least a dormant knowledge of the language.

Left: **Hotel receptionists are able to converse with tourists in fluent English.**

Opposite: **A young girl reading the Koran in classical Arabic.**

An Arabic sign at the Bahrain National Museum.

Classical Arabic is the language of the Koran and is the same throughout the Arab world. Spoken Arabic, on the other hand, varies considerably among countries and regions.

Transliteration of Arabic sounds into English can be a problem. No official transliteration exists, which explains why "Mohammed" is as correct as "Muhammad," "Muhamid," "Mohamed," and so on. Also, Arabic has 10 sounds that do not exist in English.

WRITTEN ARABIC

Arabic is written from right to left, using an alphabet invented in the fourth century. It quickly spread with the expansion of the Arabic Empire after the death of Prophet Mohammed and under the influence of Arab traders to places as distant as Turkey, Malaysia, and Indonesia, where the script was used to write indigenous languages.

The Arabic alphabet has 28 letters and is entirely phonetic, which means it is written the way it sounds. It has developed from single letters to a cursive form, where all letters in a word are joined. There are no capital letters, but each letter can change its form depending on its position in a word. Not all vowels are written.

In Bahrain calligraphy is a highly valued art, stemming from the time when the Koran was copied by hand. Calligraphers write Arabic using a reed pen with an angled point that allows bold downstrokes, narrow upstrokes, and shades of in-between.

English numerals have their origin in Arabic numbers, which in turn came from India. There is not much evident similarity today, except for numbers 1 and 9, because both systems have developed and changed over the centuries. Nonetheless, they are still known as "Arabic numerals" in English.

A wall plaque with Islamic inscription.

BODY LANGUAGE

Physical contact between people of the same sex is more frequent in Bahrain than in northern European countries and the United States. For two men, or two women, to hold hands indicates only friendly feelings and nothing more. A hand on the knee when men are talking is not an indication of homosexual advances.

On the other hand, any public display of affection across the sex line, even between husband and wife, is taboo, although it is slightly more tolerated in Bahrain compared with Saudi Arabia and Iran, where offenders are immediately pounced on and punished by the religious police. The same behavior is expected of foreigners.

Bahrainis often rub noses as a form of greeting.

In a formal setting in Bahrain, a Bahraini with a high social status awarding a diploma to a Bahraini woman may congratulate her by shaking her hand. There should be no other physical contact. Between men, however, the habit of handshakes is firmly established in Bahrain and commonly seen, although the handshake itself is unlikely to be either firm or a shake. Rather than grasp and shake in the manner common in the United States, the Bahrainis touch their right hands in a soft, sliding gesture. The handslide may often be followed by fluid moves that bring the same hand to the heart, lips, and forehead. These gestures indicate sincerity and respect.

Men and women attending a Bahraini social occasion will be physically segregated. Everybody will take off their shoes if the function takes place at home, but not if it is an official reception. More often than not, guests will cover their heads with headcloths. As a rule of thumb, the more formal the setting, the greater the coverage.

SOME COMMON ARABIC EXPRESSIONS

As a result of the widespread knowledge of the Koran among Muslim populations worldwide and the tendency for parents to give their children Islamic names (which are actually Arabic names), certain Arabic expressions are known throughout the Islamic world, which stretches beyond lands where Arabic is used as a principal language of communication. The following expressions are used all the time in Bahrain and understood by the great majority of Muslims worldwide. The English transliteration is not standard.

wa-alaykum salaam	and peace be with you
alhamdillalah	thanks be to God
bismillah	in the name of God
insha'allaah	God willing
ya allah	with God's help

NAMES

Bahrainis are proud of their heritage and ancestry, and many can trace their origins back through the male line to the time when their fore-fathers first arrived in Bahrain. Anybody with the family name Al-Khalifais is related to the emir and ruling family of Bahrain. Families of Persian origin may have surnames indicating the name of their village or neighborhood of origin in Iran.

In daily use the family name is often dropped. A person's full name consists of his or her given name plus *bin/ibn*, which means "son," or *bint*, which means "daughter," followed by the father's name. The name Ali bin Mochtar means Ali, son of Mochtar; Mochtar is not the family name.

Common names for girls include the names of the Prophet's wives and those that suggest beauty, such as Jamileh (beautiful) or Yasmina, the fragrant jasmine flower.

This form of naming reflects the importance of the father and the eldest male son in the family. A woman in Bahrain, like a woman in most Arab countries, is simply remembered as the daughter of, or the wife of, some male. The difference is that in Bahrain she retains her own father's name even after marriage. When she has succeeded in bearing her husband a son, she may graduate to *umm*, which means "mother."

The importance of the family and the need for the family to look after its own members means that adoption outside the family is almost nonexistent. Every Bahraini can name his or her lineage ancestors, and almost all Bahrainis possess a given name of a deceased family member in the father's line.

Popular names given to boys include Mohammed, Yusef (Joseph), Musa (Moses), and Abdullah.

ARTS

ISLAM PROVIDES BAHRAINIS with a way of life, including prayer and forms of artistic expression. However, it prohibits the reproduction of any creature, whether human or animal. This prohibition stems from the Islamic belief that only God can create life. By extension, an artist who makes an image—painted, carved or molded—of any living being is acting like God. To praise the work of such an artist is, in the minds of conservative Muslims, similar to worshipping an idol, which is forbidden.

Equally strong restrictions are placed on the performing arts. It is inappropriate for Bahraini men to listen to women sing or watch them dance or act. In Bahrain, however, there are women musicians who belong to some *idda* ("eed-DAH") or folk music group. The movie theaters in Manama show mostly Indian films, with much singing and dancing and some acting by both men and women.

On the other hand, live performances by Western and Arab singers and traveling theater companies, and even the occasional disco are limited to the quarantine-like premises of selected hotels. The excuse for these entertainments is that they are provided for foreign, non-Muslim guests.

Not all Islamic countries interpret art in this restrictive way, but Saudi Arabia and comparatively liberal Bahrain tend to do so. Given these traditions and the popular mindset created by such restrictions, art and sculpture tend to be abstract, and artistic expression is channeled into traditional crafts such as embroidery and weaving, religious art such as calligraphy, literary arts such as poetry, and functional arts such as the architecture of mosques, houses, and until modern shipbuilding took over, small fishing boats known as *dhows*.

Above: **At the Bahrain National Museum, tourists can find abstract art conforms to Islam, in addition to traditional religious art like calligraphy.**

Opposite: **A basket weaver practicing his trade.**

MUSICIANS

The *idda* is a traditional folk music group of 20 to 30 members, mostly women, who perform at wedding ceremonies. These performers are also employed to sing and dance at parties celebrating passages in the life cycle, such as circumcision, and during festivals such as the Eid holidays. Each occasion has its particular songs and dances. Different rhythms, known as *al-tabul* ("al-TAH-bull"), are made by beating drums of various sizes and tones. The lead singer is always a woman, and the group is named after her. The drummers are accompanied by a choir that follows the drums' rhythm with steady hand clapping. While a female band might appear somewhat alien to the prevailing religious thinking on the performing arts, the members of an *idda* maintain full Muslim propriety— they are covered from head to toe and usually veiled.

EMBROIDERY

Bahraini costumes are always beautifully embroidered. Every woman will learn this craft to some extent at home and at school. The most exquisite embroidery on the finest materials, usually imported silk, is done by professionals, women who make a living out of embroidering dresses with elaborate designs of gold and silver thread on cotton and silk.

A highly skilled embroiderer can retrieve and restore valuable old gold thread from worn clothing and rework it on an embroidery frame held steady on the knee. Almost all designs are fully in line with Islamic art, and they commonly depict flowers, stars, crescents, and geometric designs.

Embroidery is usually a woman's activity. Most women learn to sew and stitch from their mothers and in school.

CLOTH WEAVING

Gone are the days when Bahrain's cloth weavers imported the finest cotton and gold and silver thread, supplied all of Bahrain's demand, wove sail cloth for *dhows*, and still produced a sizeable surplus for export. What remains of the trade exists in a few villages, namely Bani Jamrah, Maqabah, Bu Sayb'a, and Bilad al-Qadim, where both men and women continue the traditional craft of weaving. Women prepare and dye the thread as well as measure the cloth, while men work at the large, complex looms. Each village specializes in a particular type of cloth, and while the markets of Bahrain are now full of machine-made imports, there is just sufficient demand to keep those weavers fully occupied, though not well-paid. Weaving is no longer a tourist attraction, because the villages involved are known for their conservatism and do not welcome cameras. For this reason, the National Museum has set up special sections where tourists may take photographs, leaving the talented village weavers alone to continue this traditional craft for as long as demand exists.

CALLIGRAPHY

The word "calligraphy" means beautiful writing in Greek. Calligraphy is part of mainstream Islamic art, where form and meaning merge in the poetry of the Koran. In Bahrain, as in other Muslim countries, it is possible to attend an art exhibition where every exhibit is a beautifully framed and presented picture of words and phrases from the Koran.

To a non-Muslim, it is difficult to appreciate that an audience can distinguish shades of artistic merit in the strokes of reed pens, but a Bahraini, similar to a Chinese, can value the quest for the perfect line and flow, as well as the artistic representation of the meaning of every word or phrase. For the Bahraini, however beautiful the calligraphy, the feeling obtained from seeing a work that merges the words of God with the artistic skills of a man is essentially religious in nature.

An example of Arabic calligraphy.

Storytelling is part and parcel of life in Bahrain despite the prevalence of printed publications.

POETRY

Poetry and storytelling have been considered the highest forms of art in Bahrain since pre-Islamic days. These are art forms that migrant desert peoples could carry with them in their memories, to be exhibited whenever a group of people took a break from work. Storytelling was, however, not without restrictions. Fiction was frowned on as being too similar to lying. Exaggeration, however, particularly when immortalizing the glorious deeds of a tribe, was acceptable.

Today poetry and stories in Bahrain are likely to be told by a father to his children. New contributions to this art form are limited because of the small Bahraini population and the colossal volume of Arabic literature that has been produced over thousands of years. Poetry remains a tradition that is much appreciated but is hard to master.

POTTERY

Pottery, one of the most ancient crafts in Bahrain, is now centered around A'ali village, the same location famous for its clay work during the Dilmun period. Many of the hand techniques have remained unaltered for thousands of years. In the past, potters supplied all of the domestic market and exported to neighboring countries.

Today, however, demand has dwindled because of competition from cheap imports, and the decline is compounded by a change in the Bahraini lifestyle over the years. Traditional pottery was decorative and functional. Potters made ovens, water containers, clay bowls for cooking and eating, and the hubble-bubble pipes that once filled the tea and coffee shops. Today much of the potter's work is to provide Bahrainis with souvenirs of the past and foreign tourists with souvenirs of Bahrain.

Using local clays of yellow and red, the potter creates popular items such as children's coin boxes, planters, and hubble-bubble pipes.

93

Few basket weavers now put their skills to use, although those who do so make a good living from the craft.

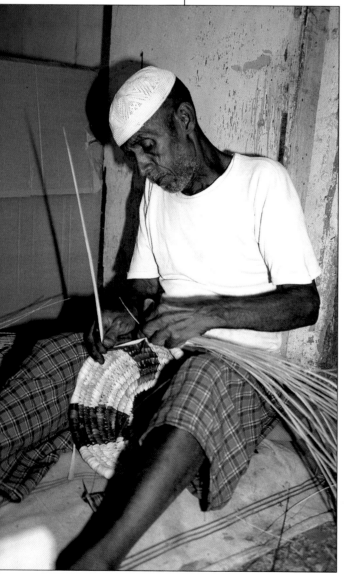

BASKETRY

The few remaining basket weavers fare well, and their traditional products are keenly sought by local people and visitors. Weavers are mostly located in the villages of Karbabad and Budaiya. Others are in Sitrah, where the rushes grow in abundance in the nearby coastal salt marshes. The basket weavers keep the craft alive and profitable, weaving the dried leaves of the date palm into baskets and dried rushes into rush mats, which provide a comfortable and practical floor covering.

TRADITIONAL HOUSES

The key features of a traditional Bahraini house are simplicity and symmetry. The outside walls have few openings and are often crowned with small turret-like forms. Light passes through an Islamic-styled, colored glass window set high over a doorway to ensure privacy. The main door presents an impressive and solid barrier to the world.

To a non-Bahraini, a house might appear fort-like and forbidding. To a Bahraini, the intricate artwork on the wooden door is a sign of welcome, and the solid walls keep out the heat of the sun and represent the comfort to be found within the closed world of the family.

The wooden architecture of an old house displays prominent Bahraini characteristics such as symmetry and turret-like structures.

The Bahraini social pattern requires a basic division of the house. There is a reception area to receive guests and serve as a family's private living space, which may be subdivided, depending on the number of nuclear families living under one roof. The traditional house is designed to accommodate families extended vertically (three or four generations) and horizontally (several brothers, their wives, and children). Each nuclear family has its individual sleeping space. There is often a communal room for the women, as well as a large kitchen area and multifunctional storerooms.

Many houses are multistoried, with each level built around the central courtyard, the principal source of air circulation and light. Within a house, generations of a single family live together and succeed one another. The house belongs to the male lineage with the eldest male as the custodian.

Modern houses tend to have more glass windows, with privacy ensured by an external fence rather than walls. If space and money permit, they are built large enough to house as many people as the traditional houses, where several related nuclear families live under one roof and take up less space than the individual houses they would otherwise occupy.

A modern house. Modern housing in Bahrain is simple in design and has few openings.

MODERN BUILDINGS

Similar to traditional houses, modern Bahraini houses are simple and symmetrical. Openings are few, except for a large and heavy main door made of carved wood. As in all Islamic architecture, the most attention is paid to the interior, reflecting the emphasis on the family unit. Rooms of family members are simple in style and furnishings, while rooms to welcome guests are usually lavishly decorated. The basic structure includes arches along corridors and arched doorways, often topped with an arched stained-glass window. Arches, niches, and stucco panels break the monotony of flat walls and create patterns of light and shade.

There are also houses near the shore used as summer retreats. Some are built with palm branches, while others have stone walls with roofs of palm branches covered with woven mats that are more suited to winter.

House walls are thick to keep the interior of the house cool in summer and warm during winter. Building materials for traditional houses are mostly found locally.

In older houses, unless a well was incorporated, there would be no water supply apart from that brought to the house daily by the water carrier. But this is seldom the case in modern Bahrain, where nearly every house has access to government-provided tap water, and most people consume desalinated water.

Modern houses of the rich resemble large villas found in wealthy areas of most developing countries. These houses retain the seclusion of the traditional houses with their high enclosures and are highly symmetrical, although here, it is the symmetry of windows rather than walls.

The landscape has changed in Bahrain. Today it is dotted with tall buildings, coastal highways, and busy causeways, and resembles the outline of tropical Singapore more than a parched Arab landscape. The architecture of the airport is remarkable. Government offices, shopping complexes, universities, and the national mosque are huge and imposing structures that reflect the shifted focus of the architect's creative expression from home to grand buildings.

LEISURE

THE WEALTH AND AMPLE FREE TIME available to Bahrainis have affected traditional patterns of leisure to some degree. The favorite activity, however, is still socializing with family, relatives, and friends. Affluence and the increase in leisure time has reinforced the traditional pattern of home-based socializing—having a foreign servant to handle the household chores, parents are able to devote more time to their children.

Beyond the family circle, entertainment is largely for foreigners. Bahrain's five cinemas cater mostly to Indians. There are 58 hotel bars that provide air-conditioned entertainment for expatriates, Saudi Arabians, and Bahrainis. Here, Bahrainis may watch concerts by Western singers and theater performances. When Bahrainis participate in leisure outside the home, they do so as a family or in a group of male relatives and friends.

Left: **Pubs like these are few in Bahrain and mostly provide entertainment for foreigners.**

Opposite: **Training a race-horse at the Equestrian and Horse-racing Club.**

The average Bahraini, although affluent, is more likely to be a spectator at a horse race than an owner because it is extremely costly to breed and raise horses.

SPORTS

Bahrainis participate in international, mostly Western, games such as soccer. The government has many plans to promote sports in the 21st century, both as a health measure and as an alternative to indolence. In 1998 the General Organization for Youth and Sports (GOYS) opened a soccer school for young men, several youth centers, and two fitness centers for women. GOYS has also helped many Bahraini sportsmen make their mark regionally and internationally in athletics, volleyball, basketball, handball, tennis, table tennis, and golf.

Equestrian and horse-racing activities are popular public spectator sports. Even in wealthy Bahrain, real participation is limited to the royal family and the richest of the rich. The Emiri Court's stable is famous as one of the oldest Arab thoroughbred stables in the Middle East.

HOTELS

The nightlife in Bahrain's hotels is known throughout the Middle East and draws many Arabs and expatriates from neighboring countries.

As Bahrain is comparatively more liberal than other Muslim countries in the Gulf, hotels serve alcoholic drinks, in principle only to non-Muslims. Occasional discos play Western music, and hotel pools display a liberal attitude toward women's attire.

Even so, participation in these forms of entertainment by Bahrainis is limited. Bahrainis prefer spectator entertainment, and this includes concerts by touring Western and Arab singers and theater performances.

Bikinis are allowed at most hotel pools, where there are fewer restrictions on a woman's dress.

PARKS AND SHOPS

Bahrain has well-kept public parks. Like other parts of the country, these parks are safe places to visit. They also provide cool shade from the scorching sun.

Bahrainis particularly like to go to parks during the cooler hours after dark. In the parks older people can relax and enjoy the fresh air and greenery, while small children have fun on the mechanical rides and other entertainment facilities.

Shopping is another collective activity Bahrainis enjoy. In Bahrain women shop more than their counterparts in many other Islamic countries, where selling and buying tend to be male activities. Whether in Bahrain

Below: **One of the shopping centers in Manama.**

Opposite: **A typical goldsmith shop in Bahrain where jewelry is openly displayed.**

or these other Islamic countries, a woman does not venture out alone. A husband accompanies his wife to the shops because she would not feel comfortable going alone. This act is not always conscious on the part of Bahrainis, who deem it natural for the family, in whole or in part, to go out together.

Shopping links Bahrainis to visitors from outside the islands more than any other activity. They have the financial means to buy anything available on the market, and Bahrain's tradition of commerce ensures that anything that does not contravene Bahrain's laws is available in the shops. Bahrain's long-established policy toward encouraging commerce through low taxes also results in cheaper prices in Bahrain than elsewhere in the Gulf.

CHILDREN'S GAMES

Children's games are gender specific. Boys are encouraged to be outgoing and competitive, and they often play away from the home. Their favorite games are usually small-boat racing and hide-and-seek.

Girls play in the home or within the courtyard. Their games often involve imitating the activities of their mothers. They also play with dolls, sing, and play hopscotch.

FESTIVALS

BAHRAIN'S RELIGIOUS FESTIVALS are dated according to the Islamic lunar calendar, while the celebration of Western New Year and Bahrain's Independence Day, celebrated on August 14, follow the Western calendar. Non-Muslims in Bahrain are free to celebrate their own festivals, but they are not necessarily granted holidays by their employers. Bahrainis of Iranian ancestry often celebrate the same festivals, although their timing and festive activities differ.

ONE-DAY HOLIDAYS

In addition to the secular holidays marking independence and the Western New Year, Bahrainis observe several one-day holidays during the Islamic year. These holidays include Prophet Mohammed's birthday, which falls

Left: **Bahrain achieved independence on August 14, 1971. National Day, however, is celebrated on December 16.**

Opposite: **Drummers playing at a festival.**

105

on the third month of the Islamic year, and the Ascension of the Prophet in the seventh month, when God took Mohammed up to heaven to view the world. These holidays inspire prayer, but because the Bahrainis do not regard them as festivals, they are not marked by large-scale public celebrations.

ISLAMIC TIME

The Islamic calendar is based on a method of measuring time that predates Islam and is still used in many countries of the world, Islamic and non-Islamic.

The year is divided into 12 months, each lasting 29 or 30 days, depending on the time between new moons. Each Islamic lunar year has 354 days instead of the more common 365 days, so events on the Islamic calendar move forward by 10 or 11 days every year when measured on the Western calendar.

As a result, festival activity is not associated with any particular season of the year, as is common in predominantly Christian countries. Bahraini festivals fall on a fixed date on the Islamic calendar but return to the same date on the Western calendar only after 32.5 years.

Islamic time began not with the birth of Prophet Mohammed, but with his flight from Mecca to Medina, calculated as A.D. 622 on the Western calendar.

EID AL-FITR

The two major holidays in Bahrain are Eid al-Fitr ("id-al-FIT-reh"), which occurs at the end of the fasting month of Ramadan, and Eid al-Adha ("id-al-ah-DAH"), the Festival of the Sacrifice, which follows about three months later.

The month of Ramadan, the ninth month of the Islamic year, is a time of directing thoughts to God and fasting in daylight hours. Until the sun sets, Muslims should not swallow anything—no food, no water, not even saliva—and should not smoke. Sexual activity is also forbidden. The sick, travelers, young children, and menstruating women are exempted from

Rifles on parade through the streets of Bahrain to celebrate Eid al-Fitr.

Juices and dates are the usual items for breaking the fast after the sun sets.

fasting, although they should try to make up for the days missed at the earliest possible date.

Ramadan starts with the sighting of the new moon, and the end of Ramadan depends on the sighting of the next new moon. If the sky is overcast, the fast continues. For this reason, it is possible in some years to find neighboring Islamic states celebrating the end of Ramadan on different days.

During the fasting month, everyone continues with their normal means of livelihood. In Bahrain those who do not work are sometimes tempted to live at night, eating large meals soon after dusk and again before dawn, and sleeping away a large part of the daylight hours. This is not considered cheating, although such a way of life does make the fast easier to endure. Many offices and businesses are open only during restricted hours during the month of Ramadan.

Collective fasting reinforces a Bahraini's identity as a Muslim. The mini-feasts that take place at dusk on every night of Ramadan strengthen the family unit. As dusk approaches, the family will sit together with glasses of water and dishes of delicacies ready, waiting for the published time or listening for the signal announcing that the sun has set.

As one family, they drink and break the fast. A hearty meal will follow, and probably another before sunrise. When Ramadan falls in the shorter, cooler days of winter, hunger and thirst are not so acute. When it falls in summer, the devout can only escape the torment by directing their thoughts to God.

The end of Ramadan is usually characterized by a slowing of life, particularly official and business life, when very little gets done. Eid al-Fitr is a religious holiday. Officially the festival lasts three days, but the unofficial celebration is longer. Eid al-Fitr may be compared to Christmas. The family celebrates together, indulges in the best of food, and visits kin and neighbors for several days, exchanging hospitality.

Business activities slow down during Ramadan when many Bahrainis leave the country to make their pilgrimage to Mecca.

Goats are commonly sacrificed during Eid al-Adha.

EID AL-ADHA

This festival celebrates the sacrifice of Abraham, who offered his son as a sacrifice because he believed that it was God's wish. God was pleased with Abraham's obedience and spared his son, replacing him with a lamb. This story is from the Old Testament, a Biblical text sanctified by Muslims as much as by Jews and Christians.

Eid al-Adha, or Festival of the Sacrifice, lasts three to four days. It coincides with the end of the *hajj* pilgrimage to Mecca, and all Muslims who can afford it sacrifice an animal, usually a goat. They will later feast on the meat and donate some of it to the poor.

In present-day Bahrain there are few poor people, therefore many Bahrainis offer a whole animal to their servants, who are usually not Muslims but are included in the festivities.

TRADITIONAL FESTIVALS

In the past Bahrainis celebrated various folk festivals related to underground fresh water and the seasonal return of the pearl-fishing boats. These festivals have dwindled because most people now drink desalinated water, and pearl-fishing has long been replaced by oil and manufacturing as the more profitable sectors of the economy.

In the place of these traditional festivals are the main Islamic festivals, which are celebrated throughout the Gulf region. While these festivals are essentially religious, they also provide an occasion for much secular fun. Important religious holidays such as Eid al-Fitr are marked by large public funfairs, which are attended by families and friends alike.

Drinking water is readily available in today's Bahrain, and this has led to the decline of traditional festivals which celebrate the presence of water.

FOOD

SOCIAL LIFE IN BAHRAIN REVOLVES around eating and the exchange of hospitality. Elaborate evening or midday meals, most often served at home, are the usual form of socializing and celebrating any occasion. Depending on the size of the gathering and the preferences of the host, Bahrainis may sit on chairs and eat with fork and spoon, or they may squat in groups on the floor and eat with the fingers of the right hand.

Regardless of the arrangements, the host has to ensure that the setting is elaborate as he can make it, that there is more food than anybody can possibly eat, and that the spread is well prepared and consists of a variety of delicious foods.

While most hospitality takes place among relatives, neighbors, and friends, foreign guests are far from excluded, and a Bahraini will feel the same obligation to provide the best for such guests.

Left: **The kitchen remains the domain of women, although those who can afford a foreign maid need not cook for the family.**

Opposite: **A buffet spread in an Arabian restaurant.**

DO'S AND TABOOS

Food is traditionally served on a carpeted floor. If a guest is present, men and women eat separately, and the children eat with either the men or the women. It is normal to serve all dishes at once and ensure replenishments are available.

Food is eaten with the right hand, even if a person is left-handed. The same applies to passing and receiving food. This is because by tradition the left hand is used for cleaning the backside after defecation. The prevalence of toilet paper has not changed this aspect of social etiquette.

Meat must be *halal* ("hah-LAL"), meaning that animals are killed in the Islamic way. The animals are blessed by God as they are drained of their blood. Bahrainis, like most other Muslims, do not eat pork as it is considered dirty or *haram* ("hah-REM") according to the Koran.

With the exception of pork, all kinds of meat are available in Bahrain's markets.

Unlike some Muslims in other countries who regard shell creatures as forbidden food, Bahrainis eat prawns and other shellfish. Shellfish have been a part of the Bahraini diet long before the introduction of Islam.

Alcohol is tolerated in Bahrain because of the large number of non-Muslim guest workers, expatriates, and tourists. Bahrainis who drink do so discreetly, and to serve food with alcohol at home is prohibited. A non-Muslim foreign guest who arrives at a Bahraini's home with a bottle of wine would place the host in a difficult position. As alcohol and pig's fat can be found in many foods, such as ice-cream, processed outside Bahrain, one has to be careful when offering gifts to a Bahraini host. The safest gift is fruit. No fruit is forbidden to a Bahraini, and any dinner party will always have a well-stocked fruit bowl. Gifts are optional when accepting a Bahraini invitation, but the guest must be careful not to unintentionally insult the host by suggesting that the food served is inadequate.

Bahrainis eat a lot and like their guests to eat more. It is good manners for dinner guests to leave after drinking coffee. Socializing in Bahrain takes place only before eating the meal and not after.

Most Bahrainis include seafood in their diet, although in other Muslim countries, shellfish, like pork, is considered *haram*.

Bahraini cuisine is a colorful assortment of international and local cuisines.

BAHRAINI FOODS

Bahraini cuisine includes a wide variety of food from many countries, including Saudi Arabia, Iran, and India, as well as from the West, rather than particular dishes unique to Bahrain. A Bahraini spread might include dahl, rice, and king prawn curry (India), mutton (Arabia), and beef steak (Western countries).

Arabian foods commonly found on Bahraini tables include *shikamba* ("SHI-kam-bah"), a creamy lamb soup with meat balls; *kofta* ("KOF-tah"), ground lamb or beef mixed with spinach, rice, spices, tomato paste, and onions; *halva* ("HEL-vah"), a very sweet dessert made from semolina or rice flour; and *shwarma* ("SHWAR-mah"), slivers of roast lamb, beef, or chicken carved from a spit.

The introduction of foreign servants and state-of-the-art kitchens and equipment have lightened the work involved in preparing the many dishes served at a Bahraini meal. The result is an expansive cuisine which is heavily influenced from abroad. Rice from India or Thailand is as

frequently eaten as bread, and the spices found in any Bahraini kitchen— cardamon, cinnamon, cloves, coriander, cumin, ginger, nutmeg, pepper, and paprika—are the result of centuries of commerce and influence.

DRINKS

Home-prepared drinks of Arabian origin are popular at any occasion. They include raisin tea, "Saudi champagne," a carbonated fruit drink, and Arab coffee flavored with cardamon.

Coffee has a special role in social interaction. Men meet at the local coffee shop to discuss events. Coffee is served to guests on arrival in a home. At the end of a meal, coffee indicates that it is time to go. Coffee cups are always filled halfway, and a guest never accepts more than three cups. After the third cup, it is good manners to hold out the empty cup, tilting it from side to side to indicate that the cup should be taken away.

Tea may be offered to guests. It is always very sweet, and the sugar is already stirred into the tea. The same three-cup rule applies.

MARKETS

Bahrain's markets used to be important to the Bahraini identity and the national economy. The most famous were various *suqs* in the major cities, where every house in a maze of narrow streets had a shopfront, and all were cozily linked together under tarpaulins stretched across the road to keep off the sun.

Walking through a *suq* is like wandering under a huge tent through an endless tunnel. To a stranger, it is easy to get lost; to the Bahraini, it is almost a comfortable extension of home. The *suq* is a place where he will meet friends and neighbors. Although many Bahrainis value the social aspects of the *suq* as much as the commercial aspects, its primary function was to be a center where Bahrainis and foreigners could buy local produce and goods imported from India, Iran, Iraq, the Arabian peninsula, and other countries.

In the past every *suq* specialized in different types of goods, and each attracted many merchants, craftsmen, peddlers, tourists, Bahrainis, and non-Bahrainis. Bahrainis also had the choice of various open-air markets held on specific days of the week at known locations. These would sell many local goods—food, pottery, mats, baskets, clothes, and song birds.

One regular market that achieved great fame among seaborne visitors was the Al Amara, one of the most important commercial centers ever in Bahrain. The Al Amara market was known for providing everything needed for the repair of ships and houses, as well as fishing and pearling equipment. The coffee houses in Al Amara were places where men gathered to talk, whether for relaxing with friends or discussing business deals with clients.

For Bahrain the *suqs* were the first and most enduring centers of international commerce, and they brought the ordinary male Bahraini in touch with people from the greater world of Islam. The *suqs* have survived to the present day, albeit in a limited, restricted way. They have become places where people living in towns and cities can exchange goods and services and enjoy a variety and quality greater than can be produced by any individual household.

Above: **Coffee houses are usually meeting places for Bahraini men, who sit and chat while smoking the hubble-bubble pipe.**

Opposite: **An open vegetable market in Bahrain.**

CONSERVATION OF THE SUQ

As in so many countries, well-stocked shopping centers and supermarkets have taken the place of traditional institutions of commerce. The wealth that came with oil has hastened the change. Bahrain's markets sold cheaply because overhead was as low as it could get. Current plans to expand high-overhead shopping complexes to cater to the ever increasing flow of tourists from across the causeway have led the Bahrain National Museum, a guardian of Bahrain's heritage, to declare the *suq* an endangered institution. To give young Bahrainis and tourists an idea of urban life in Bahrain in the years past, the Bahrain National Museum has recreated a miniature *suq* with narrow streets, blacksmiths, leather workers, goldsmiths,

Modern shopping centers and supermarkets provide a clean and comfortable way of shopping.

carpenters, tobacconists, barbers, tailors, herbalists, sweet-makers, grocers, and bakers, and of course, tea shops and coffee houses.

LAMB WITH QUINCE

This meat and fruit stew is believed to have originated, like the majority of Bahrain's population, in Persia. It spread across the Gulf to Bahrain and Arabia and is now enjoyed throughout many parts of the Middle East and even as far west as North Africa. The ingredients can be varied, for example, if quince is not available, it may be replaced by cooking apples, apricots, and hard pears.

1 large onion, chopped coarsely
2 to 3 tablespoons sunflower oil
dashes of salt and pepper
ginger, sliced
1 teaspoon cinnamon
1/2 teaspoon saffron powder
2.2 lbs (1 kg) boned leg, shoulder, or fillet of lamb, trimmed of fat and skin
1.7 lbs (750g) quinces
1/2 teaspoon powdered sugar or honey

Fry the onion in oil until soft. Cut the meat into square chunks and add to the onion in the frying pan. When the meat is brown all over, add salt, pepper, ginger, cinnamon, and saffron powder. Pour in the tomatoes, cover with water, and simmer for an hour until meat is tender. Wash and core the quinces, cut into four or eight pieces (depending on size), and add to the stew. Cook until the quinces soften, which should take about 10 to 30 minutes. You may add the juice of half a lemon and some powdered sugar or honey if desired. Serve hot on a flat dish, garnishing the lamb with the quinces and the remaining sauce from the pot. Accompany with rice or bread.

Bahraini cuisine reflects the islands' location and history. Seafood is popular and plentiful, as are spices and seasoning, brought to Bahrain's shores by Arabian and Persian traders.

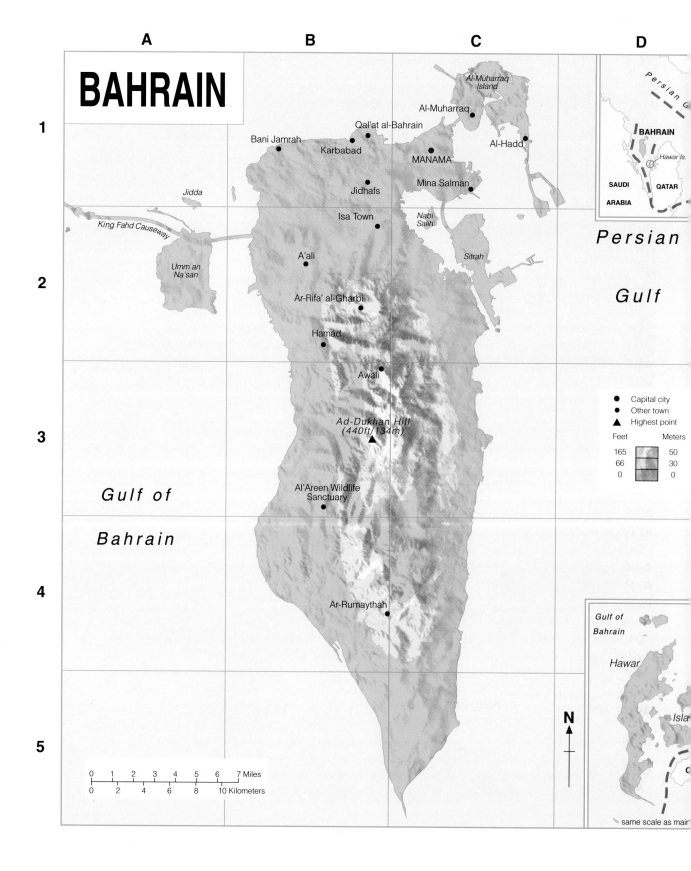

BAHRAIN

A **B** **C** **D**

1

Al-Muharraq Island

Al-Muharraq

Qal'at al-Bahrain

Bani Jamrah

Karbabad

MANAMA

Al-Hadd

Jidhafs

Mina Salman

Jidda

Isa Town

Nabi Salih

King Fahd Causeway

Umm an Na'san

A'ali

Sitrah

2

Ar-Rifa' al-Gharbi

Hamad

Awali

Ad-Dukhan Hill
(440ft/134m)
▲

3

Al'Areen Wildlife Sanctuary

Gulf of

Bahrain

4

Ar-Rumaythah

Persian

Gulf

● Capital city
● Other town
▲ Highest point

Feet		Meters
165		50
66		30
0		0

Persian G

BAHRAIN

Hawar Is.

SAUDI
ARABIA

QATAR

Gulf of Bahrain

Hawar

Isla

same scale as mair

N
↑

0 1 2 3 4 5 6 7 Miles
0 2 4 6 8 10 Kilometers

5

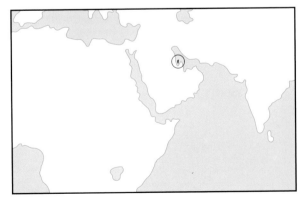

QUICK NOTES

OFFICIAL NAME
State of Bahrain

LAND AREA
239 square miles (620 square km)

CLIMATE
Arid, with mild, pleasant winters and very hot, humid summers

NATURAL RESOURCES
Groundwater, oil, natural harbors

CAPITAL
Manama

ADMINISTRATIVE DIVISIONS
12 municipalities, all administered from Manama

HIGHEST POINT
Ad-Dukhan Hill (440 feet / 134 m)

POPULATION
629,090 (July 1999 estimate), of which 36% or 227, 801 are non-Bahrainis

ETHNIC GROUPS
Bahraini (63%), Asian (13%), Iranian (8%), other Arab (10%), others (6%)

NATIONAL LANGUAGE
Arabic

LANGUAGE OF COMMERCE
English

MAJOR RELIGION
Islam (70% Shiites and 30% Sunnis)

MINORITY RELIGIONS
Christian, Jewish, Hindu, Parsee

CURRENCY
Bahraini dinar (BD)
US$1 = BD 0.377 (April 2000)

MAIN INDUSTRIES
Oil processing and refining, aluminum smelting, offshore banking, tourism

MAJOR TRADING PARTNERS
Saudi Arabia, India, United States, Japan, United Arab Emirates

GOVERNMENT
Absolute monarchy

LEGAL SYSTEM
Based on Islamic law and English common law

POLITICAL LEADERS
Emir H.H. Sheikh Hamad Bin Isa Al-Khalifa
Prime Minister H.H. Sheikh Khalifa Bin Salman Al Khalifa
Crown Prince Salman bin Hamad Al-Khalifa

INDEPENDENCE DAY
August 15, 1971

NATIONAL DAY
December 6 (1971)

GLOSSARY

al-khataba ("al-KAH-tah-bah")
A marriage broker, usually female.

al-tabul ("al-TAH-bull")
Different rhythms made by beating drums.

daffa ("DAH-fah")
A long overgarment that covers the head and opens at the front.

Eid al-Adha ("id-al-ah-DAH")
Festival of sacrifice.

Eid al-Fitr ("id-al-FIT-reh")
The end of the fasting month.

Hadith ("ha-DEEH")
A book containing the sayings of Prophet Mohammed.

Hajj ("HAJJ")
Muslim's pilgrimage to Mecca.

halal ("hah-LAL")
Food Muslims are permitted to eat.

halva ("HELL-vah")
A dessert made from semolina or rice flour.

haram ("hah-REM")
Foods that are considered dirty and forbidden to Muslims.

idda ("eed-DAH")
Traditional folk musicians, usually female.

imam ("ee-MAHM")
The religious leader of a Muslim community.

kofta ("KOF-tah")
Ground lamb or beef mixed with spinach, rice, spices, tomato paste, and onions.

Koran ("KOH-ran")
The holy book of Islam.

milfa ("MILL-fah")
A black rectangular piece of net-like cotton worn on the head

Shariah ("SHAR-ri-yah")
Islamic law.

Shiite Islam
An Islamic school of thought. Shiite Muslims broke away from the main group after Prophet Mohammed died.

shikamba ("SHI-kam-bah")
A creamy lamb soup with meat balls.

shwarma ("SHWAR-mah")
Slivers of roast lamb, beef, or chicken carved from a spit.

Sunni Islam
An Islamic school of thought. It is also the main group of Muslims in the world.

suq ("SOOK")
Permanent markets.

BIBLIOGRAPHY

Ali Akbar Bushiri. *Dilmun Culture*. Manama: National Council for Culture, Arts and Literature, 1992.

Bahrain in Figures. Manama: Directorate of Statistics, November 1997.

Bahrain, Island of Opportunities. Manama: Ministry of Labor and Social Affairs, 1999.

Bahrain, The Road to Progress. Manama: Ministry of Cabinet Affairs and Information, 1998.

Bahrain 21st Century. Manama: Khaleej Times Supplement, November 12, 1997.

The Temple Complex at Barbar. Manama: Ministry of Information, 1996.

Sami A. Hanna. *A Modern Cultural History of Bahrain*. Manama: National Council for Culture, 1999.

INDEX

INDEX

INDEX